Tales of the
OLD GAMEKEEPERS

Brian P. Martin

Tales of the
OLD GAMEKEEPERS

David & Charles

To Cecil Buckingham (1904–88),
the first keeper I ever met.
He came, like a ghost, out of the woods.

Old Brock – the night watcher's companion

· ·

British Library Cataloguing in Publication Data

Martin, Brian P.
  Tales of the old gamekeepers
  1. Great Britain, Gamekeeping
  I. Title
  639.9′5′0941

  ISBN 0-7153-9232-8

Colour illustrations by Philip Murphy except p2 by Will Garfit

First published 1989   Reprinted 1989
Reprinted 1990 (twice)   Reprinted 1991 (three times)
Reprinted 1992 (twice)   Reprinted 1993 (twice)
Reprinted 1994   Reprinted 1995   Reprinted 1996

Typeset by Typesetter (Birmingham) Ltd
Smethwick, West Midlands
and printed in England
by Butler & Tanner Ltd, Frome
for David & Charles
Brunel House   Newton Abbot   Devon

CONTENTS

The Dead Gamekeeper   6

Introduction   8

Overcoming Tyranny · *Charles South*   16

The World's Oldest Keeper? · *George Pryke*   26

Brideshead Revisited · *Stanley Ware*   30

Their Majesties' Keeper · *Jack Clark*   41

Mainly from the Archives   48

King of the Gamekeepers · *Harry Grass*   65

From Bird Scarer to Headkeeper · *Len Macey*   74

Last of the Line · *Wally Fakes*   83

The One-Estate Man · *Bill Gill*   90

Mainly from the Archives   96

Everyone called me 'Foxy' · *Frank Hunt*   113

Good Times, Hard Times · *Harry Ward*   125

Mainly from the Archives   130

Honest as the Day's Long · *Harry Churchill*   146

Mainly from the Archives   160

The Farmer's Boy · *Leslie Buckle*   172

Index   185

THE DEAD GAMEKEEPER

Earth now holds him in her rooty snare
  beneath the rat-run sycamore;
far is fur and feather from his care,
  another watcher lifts his door.

Now vermilion-fanged the vermin dare
  creep out from fosse and fen and cave;
and the wild hawks on the flowing air
  poise and pass above his grave.

ANON

in Snapdragon, 6 December 1924

The keeper's perks

INTRODUCTION

In writing this book I have become increasingly aware of my audacity in attempting to 'précis' the lives of such great countrymen. Each one is worthy of a book in his own right and all I have been able to do is highlight their remarkably long labours and loves. Therefore I must begin with an apology to them all, and to their families, for my expediency in cramming them into one publishable package.

The reminiscences of men aged 65 to 95 comprise the nucleus of this book, and if there is one thing my research has taught me it is respect for my elders; and this experience has impressed upon me just how fleeting are man's years on this ever-changing earth. At the same time I have been surprised how sharp the memory of boyhood can remain down the long years. Of course, we all remember the milestones and important dates in our lives, but I doubt if many people can recapture the details of old English country life as these men have.

I have been both spellbound and envious in learning of the unspoilt countryside – lost forever – of hedgerows teeming with partridges and glades ablaze with wild flowers. But I have also been angry at the abuse of these men by many who should have known better, and sympathetic at their deprivation and hardship.

Men have always said that, like the poet, the keeper is born and not made, and in this a certain amount of truth still remains. The basic qualities required have always been great loyalty, genuine concern for fellow men and a detailed knowledge and love of the countryside and natural history. But early keepering was often an extension of serfdom in which the under-privileged worked incredibly hard to satisfy the whims of sometimes ungrateful and ignorant masters. Fortunately, we have come far this century and at long last most keepers do not need to touch their forelocks quite so much. The subjects of my books have witnessed tremendous improvements in pay and conditions of service, but they have often had to fight every inch of the way to overcome the pomposity and selfishness of a minority who have literally inherited the earth.

That said, it must be emphasised that in my experience and in that of the keepers written about here, the majority of employers have on the whole been both kind and generous. How else could they have inspired such loyalty and in some cases retained their keepers for their entire working lifetimes? Today the only real bar to progress is in the difficulty of obtaining a sensible wage for the number of hours put in. Sadly, as in all occupations concerned with the countryside, the keeper seems to be penalised for actually enjoying his work! As always, the answer is: 'If you aren't happy you are free to leave. There are a hundred others eager to take over from you.'

Almost without exception, the keepers I visited said that they would certainly 'do it all over again'. They have welcomed advances in keepering techniques and not

Glades ablaze with flowers . . .

hesitated in waving goodbye to the labour-intensive system of rearing under broody hens. But at the same time they often condemn modern keepers as 'mere poultry farmers' and criticise them for lack of knowledge in country ways. Gone are the endless hours of food preparation and trapping to protect wild nests, only to be replaced by excessive reliance on rearing and release. Despite more and more people injecting cash into the sport, however, the overall trend is towards smaller bags of high quality and undoubtedly the keeper of the 1990s will need to know as much about habitat management as his grandfather did.

One thing that has remained constant has been the gamekeeper's standing in the country community – friend of prince and pauper and the confidant of everyone, enjoying the respect of both humble village folk and landed gentry. More than once has a famous politician sought the honest opinion of his keeper on some sensitive public or private issue, and often has the farm labourer turned to his friend the keeper in his hour of need. In no other occupation has a man ever needed to get on with so many people from all walks of life.

Most of the men whose lives I invaded have worked for rich, powerful men – some household names – at some stage of their lives, and it is to their great credit that they have resisted the temptation to 'spill the beans'. But this inevitably

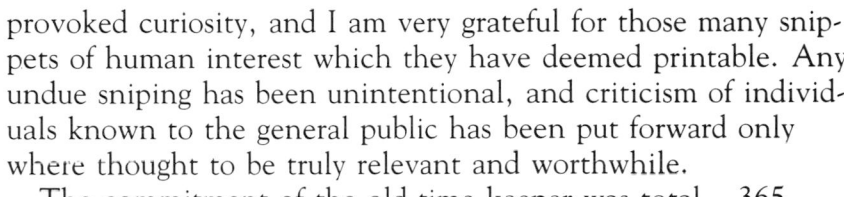

provoked curiosity, and I am very grateful for those many snippets of human interest which they have deemed printable. Any undue sniping has been unintentional, and criticism of individuals known to the general public has been put forward only where thought to be truly relevant and worthwhile.

The commitment of the old-time keeper was total – 365 days a year and often twenty-four hours a day in all weathers, nightwatching or on the rearing field, with the constant threat of injury or even death at the hands of vicious poachers. Before the advent of the motor car, access to the majority of shoots in remote rural areas was difficult, so most poachers were local men with whom the keeper played a perpetual game of cat and mouse. And in dealing with many poor people struggling to support large families he did have some sympathy. But today all is different and the old-fashioned 'one-for-the-pot' man has been replaced by highly mobile gangs of thugs who stop short of nothing. It was inevitable that tales of poaching should occupy so many of these pages, but they do illustrate very well the evolution of society's attitude towards offenders. In this, as in everything, I have let the keepers tell the tales in their own words wherever possible.

Unfortunately, even the oldest keeper – 95-year-old George Pryke of Shropshire – cannot recall the earliest days of game-shooting so I have also drawn on wide-ranging literature to paint a picture of keepering life beyond memory. In this I am particularly indebted to *Shooting Times and Country Magazine*, the weekly journal which has entertained sporting men every week since 1882. Its launch coincided with the beginning of the so-called 'golden age' of shooting when, in the years up to World War I, a vast army of gamekeepers was employed. Since then their number has steadily diminished as costs have risen and techniques have become more efficient. Thus today we have a mere three or four thousand keepers in full-time employment.

I am also grateful to my informants for the loan of photographs which they have cherished from early days. These have provided a fascinating contrast with the pictures I have taken of the keepers in retirement today.

Finally, may I say thank you to all the men who have divulged so much detail about their private lives, and to their wives whose cooking was inevitably something not to be missed. But special as these folk are, they are not alone. Dotted across the land in quiet country cottages are other great characters with similar stories to tell, and I humbly beg their pardon for not having had the time to visit them and the space to immortalise them all in print.

I was just seven years old when I first met a gamekeeper, and I was very much in the wrong. Trying to work out how to reach some sand-martin nests and eggs in the face of a disused gravel working, I had not noticed the tall, gaunt figure in a great-coat creep up on me from nearby woods. It was Cecil Buckingham who, many years later, was to be the subject of my first-ever magazine article, printed in *Gamekeeper and Countryside* magazine.

Cecil died in 1988 at the age of eighty-four, and good health had enabled him to continue the profession of his father and grandfather into old age. Born in 1904, he did not choose his career, for even while still at school he was being drilled by his father in pheasant rearing and country lore.

His birthplace was the 20,000-acre (8,094ha) Merton estate, near Stanford village in Norfolk, where he remembered seven Guns shooting 1,600 pheasants in one day. His vivid memories recaptured how the wind, blowing strongly across the dry, flat land, often produced small sandstorms, after which he would find 'Half the field up in the hedge'.

He told me 'Lord Walsingham often had between eighty and a hundred beaters, but was very particular about dogs not runnin' about all over the place'.

For Cecil, full-time estate work started at the age of twelve and a half, when an official, written application was required from his employer because the normal school leaving age was fourteen, or thirteen if you were lucky and had a job to go to. His starting wage was 6s 6d a week; his father was earning 17s a week plus one suit of clothes a year. And there was no rent to pay, so then the gamekeeper was generally better off than the average farm labourer.

As 'dog boy', Cecil was responsible for feeding and exercising the dogs and ferrets. Hand-rearing pheasants came later, when he took over his father's job. 'The food is all out of a bag now, but then you have to have light hands to be a mixer – just like a woman mixing a cake', he said. As we spoke, he stooped to toss a log on the fire, then remembered that they would add saffron root to the food mix. 'It helped the head feathers, and if you got the head feathers to come properly, then the bird was thriving, like a child when he gets his teeth.' Overfeeding was almost a crime, and his father would come round to check on young Cecil. 'He would rub his foot on the ground and listen for the crunch of dry grain husks.'

February 1 was a red-letter day for Cecil and all the other keepers. It was the end of the shooting season and the day when the tips box from 'the big house' was opened, and the contents shared. Sometimes, of course, donations were entrusted to the headkeeper and unfortunately 'some were more honest than others'. Occasionally tips were given direct to the underkeepers so there was always 'keen competition to get up front'. Many family men relied considerably on these tips, as some do to this day.

Cecil was lucky to find a local position, as 'in a new job they'd rather you came a hundred miles. You had to be an honest man – conscientious'. There was always a suspicion that local men, being friends, would sometimes aid and abet each other to cheat the estate or become over-familiar with local poachers.

Keeper's cottage

ROYAL AGRICULTURAL HALL - LONDON

CRUFT'S

GREAT INTERNATIONAL DOG SHOW

WEDNESDAY FEB. 9TH

THURSDAY FEB. 10TH

THE GREATEST DOG SHOW the World has ever seen for

SPORTING DOGS

SPECIAL CLASSES RESERVED FOR GAMEKEEPERS

GAMEKEEPER'S ASSOCIATION hold their ANNUAL SHOW
FEBRUARY 9 and 10   ::   Entries close January 24th

Judge for Gamekeepers' Classes   Mr. S. J. LING

I must go to Crufts!

IT'S THE GAMEKEEPERS SHOW

THE DOGS WILL BE BENCHED AND FED BY SPRATT'S PATENT LTD.

When Cecil apprehended me in my home town of Gosport, on the Hampshire coast, he lived on a 'green island'. He had been keeper there when 2,000 fine estate acres (810ha) spread from Fort Brockhurst to Stubbington Lane, but as so-called development ate away at the land his patch was reduced to only 40 acres (16ha), floating in a sea of council and naval-quarters concrete. When Gosport Borough Council purchased this outstanding reserve of ancient oakwood, marsh and heath, known locally as the 'Wildgrounds', he was retained as its warden. He continued to live in the 200-year-old cottage at Rowner, Gosport, into which the family had moved in 1919, when Cecil was 14. Eventually he took over from his father on the estate which had been in the Prideaux-Brune family since the thirteenth century.

In many ways I felt sorry for this very proud man. How sad it was that someone who had known the prime of gameshooting in unspoilt Norfolk on one of the country's most celebrated estates – and later in Hampshire – should end his days chasing joy-riding motor cyclists through the woods on his rickety old push-bike. It was like the nineteenth century trying to catch up with the twentieth, but being left further and further behind. Yet there is no doubt that his weathered, and in some ways noble countenance, fired my imagination and encouraged a lifetime's devotion to outdoor pursuits: for that I remain forever in his debt.

BRIAN MARTIN
Brook, Surrey

Wild nests were carefully guarded

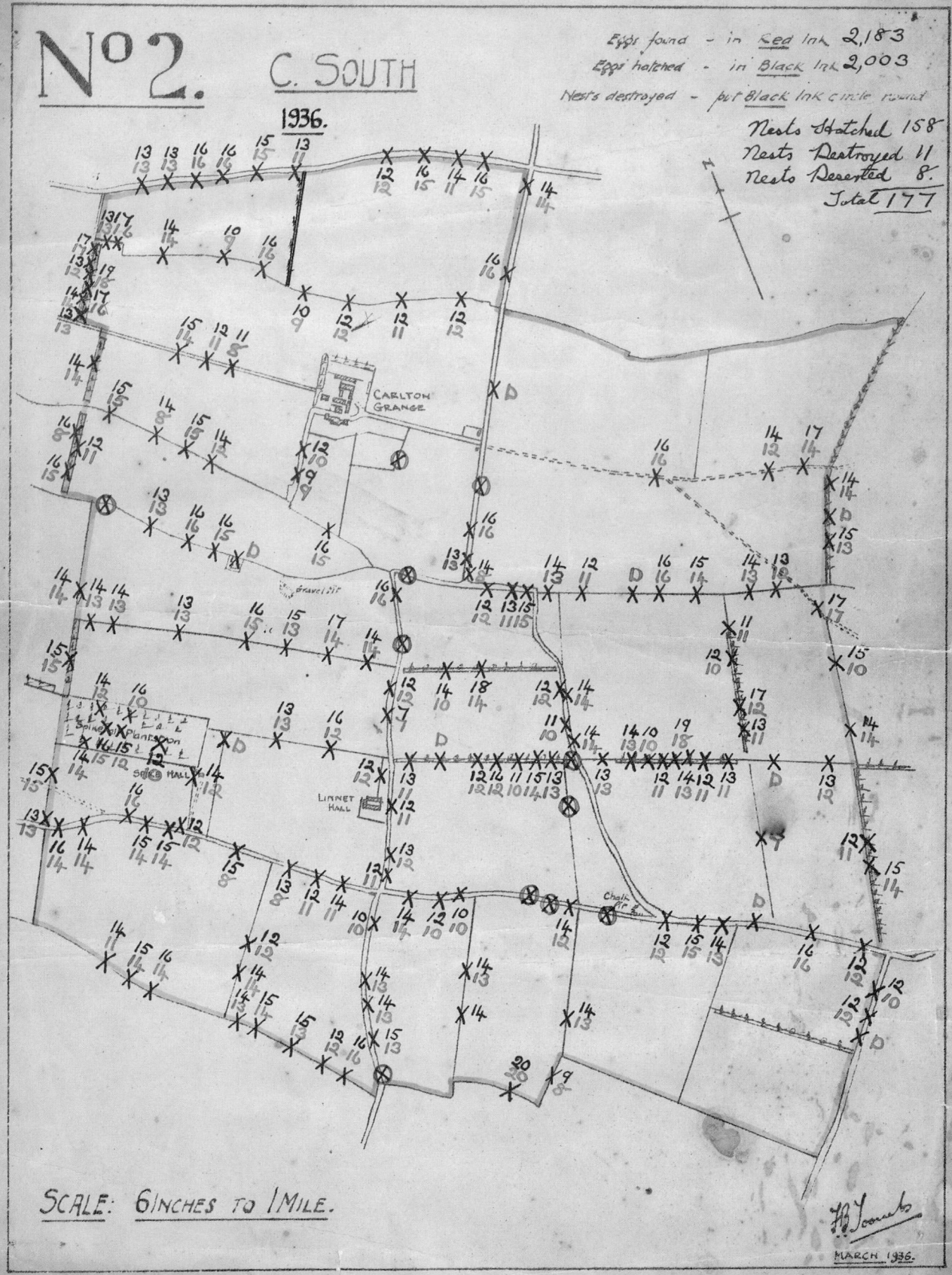

N°2.

C. SOUTH

1936.

Eggs found – in Red Ink 2,183
Eggs hatched – in Black Ink 2,003
Nests destroyed – put Black Ink circle round

Nests Hatched 158
Nests Destroyed 11
Nests Deserted 8.
Total 177

CARLTON GRANGE

Gravel Pit

Spinney Plantation

SPIKE HALL

LINNET HALL

Chalk Pit Farm

SCALE: 6 INCHES TO 1 MILE.

H.B. Toombs

MARCH 1936.

CHARLES SOUTH

Windsor, Frensham (Surrey) and Six Mile Bottom (Cambridgeshire)

Despite starting his career under one of the most tyrannical headkeepers this century, Charles South went on to become one of the most successful and respected exponents of his profession. But even now Charlie remembers bitterly every detail of that cruel regime at Windsor Great Park back in the Twenties.

Born on 10 November 1908 at Rushton, Hertfordshire, Charlie grew up in a keepering family. His father was a single-handed keeper for Major M. E. Barclay, who was Master of the Puckeridge Foxhounds (his son, Captain C. G. E. Barclay, is still Joint Master of the Puckeridge & Thurlow), and in 1921 became underkeeper at the famous Six Mile Bottom Estate near Newmarket, where eventually Charlie would make his mark.

However, when Charlie left school his father said he would be better off mole trapping and advised him to get six dozen traps to make a start. This he did, catching about forty moles a week and selling their skins for 5d each. In addition, he went beating at Six Mile Bottom and on the celebrated neighbouring estates of Stetchworth and Dullingham for 7s a day and a pint of beer, 'but we had to take our own lunch'.

At the age of fifteen he became woodman for Six Mile Bottom at 26s a week, and continued in the post till he was nineteen, when his father took him to Crufts to get him a keepering job, the famous show acting as a sort of keepers' clearing house in the old days.

At Crufts Charlie met the headkeeper of Windsor Great Park, and thus began 'the worst year of my life. E. R. Dadley was to prove a real ogre. He was a right bugger and got me there under false pretences. I was supposed to be a keeper's help but spent all my time milking cows, sawing wood, gardening, looking after chickens and pigs, and even growing mangel-wurzels for the cattle – bloody slavery.'

His pay was 36s a week, but out of this he had to pay a guinea for his lodgings, and he was not given any special clothes. 'The proper keeper then had 37s 6d a week plus one suit of clothes a year.

'Just about the first words he said to me were: "No drinking and no smoking, and if I ever catch you off the estate you'll get a minute's notice." We even had to ask permission to get a haircut, and when this was given we had to be back in double-quick time.'

Charlie South's 1936 map, signed by the estate's agent Toombs, of the Spike Hall Beat at Six Mile Bottom. It marks the locations of all the partridge nests and gives full details of their success or failure. At the time most keepers were required to make such maps and they had to be most accurate as they were subject to spot checks by headkeepers or employers

Young Charlie South overcame a great deal of hardship during the early part of his career

At Windsor Charlie was one of six helps for fourteen underkeepers, and there were two deerkeepers and a boy to help them, as well as a groom, 'all under the demon Dadley'. Together they reared some 20,000 pheasants each season.

'Nobody liked Dadley: he got through sixty underkeepers and helps in just ten years – they just couldn't stick it. Yet he came highly recommended from the famous Hall Barn shoot in Buckinghamshire, which had the record for the number of pheasants shot in a day.' Of course, both Edward VII and George V often went shooting at Lord Burnham's Hall Barn and must have been impressed by Dadley's performance there.

'But the birds were always very poor at Windsor. The Prince of Wales – later Edward VIII – said that shooting there was "like knocking off chickens" and wanted no part of it.'

In July and August, when the young birds were put to wood, Charlie had to take his turn at nightwatching, one night in three. 'The first time, I went to relieve the underkeeper between Sandpit Gate and Ascot racecourse for a 10pm to 6am stint. After that I went straight home and said to the underkeeper with whom I lodged, next door to the headkeeper, "I'll have a nice cup of tea and go straight to bed now". But he said "Oh no you don't – you still have to do your normal work". So I carried on and did two days and a night with no bed. I can tell you I was mighty tired and nearly fell asleep over my spade when I tackled a bit of digging. But we did get an extra half-crown a night for watching.

'Talking about money, there was just one occasion when Dadley showed a spark of humanity. After I'd been at Windsor a while I was summoned to the office to get my travelling expenses from Six Mile Bottom to Windsor. I had come via Liverpool Street and Paddington and along the way had to pay five shillings for a taxi. Well, Major Taylor, the clerk, said "You should have gone on the Underground for tuppence". But blow me if Dadley didn't stick up for me. He was furious and banged his bowler hat down on the table, saying to Major Taylor: "Would you go on the Underground with a great tin trunk like his, and all the other gear, and not really knowing where you were going?" At that the Major gave me the full 15s to cover the whole journey without further question.

'At Windsor there wasn't really any way we could slip out the gate past Dadley, but one of my mates said it was safe to get out and in when the pips went on the radio as then we knew he was busy listening to the news. He never missed it. But we had to be ever so careful as Dadley was really crafty. He would gallop off on his grey horse at six in the morning to see two or three keepers and sometimes turn back within half-an-hour to surprise them, to see if they were smoking or sitting in the cab.

'One of the jobs Dadley's groom and me had to do was harrow down the very high bracken with the horses to make a clearing where the coops would go. Doing this we used to catch loads of rabbits, hitting them on the head with sticks as they all concentrated in the last little bit of cover. We were supposed to sell them to the butcher and give the proceeds to the estate, but we soon learned that the milkman wanted them for sixpence each.

'Another example of Dadley's vicious streak was when I had a whitlow and had to go on my bike to visit the doctor at Winkfield, who put my arm in a sling and told me I was very run down – I'd lost a stone in three months. But when I went back that swine Dadley snatched the sling off and told me I was skiving.

'Another time he told me to milk a cow till it was really dry and then take it on a lead to Bracknell Market – seven miles away! So off I went through the forest, and before long the wretched thing had thrown me over a few times. But enough was enough. I managed to get the beast over and then it behaved itself.

'Anyway, I got there in the end, and for all my trouble Dadley had given me just one shilling – exactly the right amount to buy a pint of beer for myself and one for Ward the groom who was sent to pick me up in a pony and cart.

'Perhaps the last straw came when I was counting the game into the larder. One day I made it 1,104 and Dadley said "You are wrong – it's one less than 1,100". When I protested he said: "What do you know – you're just a boy", and I had to do it all over again. It was still exactly 1,104, but do you know, he never apologised.

'So I gave a month's notice and Dadley said I could change my mind at any time. But he did also say that he would try to get me another job, so off we went to Crufts again. As a result I ended up going to Frensham Park in Surrey, to work as beatkeeper for Richard Combe of the brewers Watney, Combe and Reed. He was really tickled by my name being Charlie South as he already had a second gardener called Charlie North and a farm labourer called Charlie West. Now, he said, he would look for a Charlie East "to get the full set".

'This was a much better job altogether. I had thirty-eight bob a week to start and this soon rose to £2, plus a suit of clothes a year and wonderful lodgings – within a few months I'd put that stone back on again. It was a far cry from Windsor, where I had only bread and marge and beetroot for supper, and where the only time we had meat was when a deer was run over once or twice a year.'

At Frensham the three keepers reared only 800 pheasants each year and some three or four hundred were shot over about three days. 'But there was plenty of duck shooting on Frensham Little Pond. However, one day when we were out in a boat Mr Combe nearly shot me in the head: it frightened him so much he declared "No more" and we all went home.

'There was also the traditional Boxing Day coot shoot on Frensham Big Pond. Anyone could go, even working men, as long as they paid the five shillings each. We shot scores and scores between us. The coots were very numerous at all seasons and during an open winter the water was sometimes fairly black with them.

'The Guns, a score or more, would assemble at the pond hotel and about half would go in boats in line to drive the pond while the rest were posted ashore. The total bag was usually about 150 plus a few duck. The "fixture" was discontinued after December 1931.'

Charlie thoroughly enjoyed his two and a half years at Frensham, but it came to an end when his father died – when he went home for the funeral he was offered his father's job at Six Mile Bottom. But this was in November, at the height of the shooting season and a difficult time to move, so the Frensham headkeeper told Charlie 'You'll have to get me a replacement before you go'. In those days keepers were few and far between in Surrey, but fortunately Charlie had a brother interested in the position. 'I wrote to him on the Hog's Back and he gladly took the job, staying there for eight years.'

Thus it was at the age of twenty-one that Charlie returned to Six Mile Bottom, to take over the Weston Colville beat, 'thick woods and heavy land, not a good part of the estate'. The heavy land was a great disadvantage as wild partridges were then the main interest and they always thrive best on light, well-drained land. But since then, that part of the estate has been sold off.

Charlie's first main task was tackling the considerable vermin problem and he caught twenty foxes in his first year. He followed a tip from an old Hampshire keeper and 'put out a bed of six gins with a stinkin' ol' cat in the middle of 'em'.

Partridge nests had to be checked religiously, of course, and in this a headkeeper would usually check up on his underkeepers – so would an interested employer. Remarkably, Charlie still has two of his maps from the 1930s, each recording details such as the number of eggs laid in each nest, number hatched etc. Proudly he recalls the day when his headkeeper and employer, Capt Cunningham-Reid, came round in the Rolls Royce to check on his records. 'Right', said the Captain, 'according to this map there should be a nest under that telegraph pole.' And there was. He then proceeded to check just three more nests, and without further ado departed, satisfied that all was in order. The beat was obviously in the hands of a competent man.

Poaching was not a great problem in this very rural area until just after the war when food was rationed and, as Charlie said, 'everyone was really hungry'. The proliferation of cars aggravated the situation, but the keepers took the registration numbers and passed them on to the police to secure many convictions. Charlie used to carry a knuckle duster in his pocket, though he never actually used it. When he was given it by another, older keeper it still had two spikes on it, but Charlie decided to file these off in case he got into trouble with the law.

Charlie's reputation grew steadily and in 1950 he was made headkeeper on the retirement of Coot, then in charge of nine men. In those days Six Mile Bottom was a private shoot and there was a constant stream of guests for Charlie to look after – 'we had over a hundred one season'.

I asked Charlie which of the many guest Guns had been his favourites. Quick as a flash and with a knowing grin, he replied: 'The ones who gave me the most money'.

Charlie South still has the knuckle duster he used to carry for protection, though he never needed to use it

CHIEF OF THE DEFENCE STAFF
MINISTRY OF DEFENCE
STOREY'S GATE, LONDON S.W.1
TELEPHONE WHITEHALL 7000

30th November 1960

Dear South,

I feel I must write to congratulate you on the fabulous shoot which we had last Saturday when we killed 1,425 pheasants.

Not only must this be a record, at all events for recent years, but practically all the birds flew very high and were so beautifully driven that they came over at such regular intervals, and if we had all shot as well as Lord Brabourne (who got 335 pheasants himself) the bag would certainly have exceeded 2,000.

It will now be the aim of Grass and myself to compete with you at Broadlands.

yours sincerely

Mountbatten of Burma

Letter from the late Earl Mountbatten of Burma to Charlie South at Six Mile Bottom, just one of a drawerful of treasured thankyou letters from appreciative guest Guns

Charlie South on the rearing field at Six Mile Bottom (John Marchington)

23

Among the most famous visitors was prolific novelist Barbara Cartland, who often came to watch her two sons (McCorquodales) shoot. 'She spent most of her time feeding Lord Louis (Mountbatten) chocolates', said Charlie's wife, Dorcas. 'She was a great talker and very familiar with all the guests.' Mrs South still has the signed books which the novelist insisted on giving her, 'but when she asked me about them I had to admit that I had not read them'.

Like other headkeepers, Charlie also accompanied his boss to many other shoots, to act as loader. 'The best I ever went to was Helmsley in Yorkshire, with Mr Noel, the Captain's son and present owner. Noel had thirty-inch guns and full-load cartridges as well as all the gear you could want, yet still found shooting difficult there. They didn't kill one in seven between them. The birds were so high you could hear the pellets rattling their wings as they flew on unscathed. And one of the other guests – Sir Kenneth Keith, a really good Shot – said "I'm giving up, I can't hit anything". The Helmsley shoot was then run by Prince Radziwill and Lord Ashburton, and didn't they spend some money on it and their guests!'

On another occasion Charlie loaded for Lord Brackley at Stetchworth. 'I was twenty-four and he was just nineteen. He had a set of three 16-bores and the headkeeper told me "You take 1 and 3 and leave 2 for Lady Alice as she likes to use that one". Mr Jolly also said "Look, he's very shy, so if he doesn't talk to you then don't talk to him". Well, this young man shot well, but sure enough, by lunchtime we had not spoken a single word. In the afternoon he continued to shoot well and in the evening I cleaned his guns, as was the custom. But do you know, we never exchanged a word all day – extraordinary. However, after the war I had occasion to load for him again, and then he did speak.

'One of my most memorable shooting days was when I had the pleasure to load for Edward Douglas-Home, brother of the famous playwright William. To my great surprise he shot a hundred cock pheasants and never missed one: that was some shooting, I can tell you.'

Charlie still has many of his old keeper's record books, from which he would transfer details of the Guns and bags to the main estate gamebooks, and also a great sheaf of thank-you letters from guest Guns, including the late Lord Louis Mountbatten. His excellent and loyal service has been well recognised by the estate and he still lives rent-free in one of the spacious, modern houses provided for estate pensioners. Well provided for, he is surrounded by shooting mementoes, including the silver plate which he was given on retirement. It is inscribed: 'Given to Charles South, headkeeper of Six Mile Bottom, in appreciation of half a century of outstanding work and for his humour and friendship. February 1974.' It is signed by his ex-boss, Noel Cunningham-Reid, and the four underkeepers.

Charlie South remains extremely alert to the ever-changing world around him and has undoubtedly been one of the most successful and best liked keepers of this century. How lucky the sport is that headkeeper Dadley of Windsor did not not kill the spirit which fired Charlie so.

Note: Sadly, Charlie South died in October, 1993.

Deservedly enjoying his retirement, Charlie South in his Six Mile Bottom garden, 1988

George Pryke
Shropshire

When 24-year-old George Pryke had 'a dose of gas' in the Somme towards the end of World War I, he never in his wildest dreams imagined that he would be fit enough to continue full-time keepering into his ninety-fifth year. Yet he did just that, with great distinction, despite having his hearing permanently damaged by shell-fire and experiencing increasingly frequent dizzy spells in which his mind 'goes blank and whirls round and round'.

Born on 18 December 1893, at Condover, three miles from Shrewsbury in Shropshire, George followed the profession of his father, who began keepering in Norfolk, became beat keeper at Acton Burnell, Shropshire, and was later headkeeper for Colonel Witmore at Dudmaston Hall, Battlefield, Shropshire.

George left school at the age of fourteen, and did 'a bit of rabbiting and post work – deliveries and so on' before starting under his father at Dudmaston at the age of fifteen. There, three keepers reared just six or seven hundred pheasants, although most of George's work was on the main partridge beat. The estate's 6,000 acres (2,428ha) were mainly arable, but 'some farms were very hungry on the sand and there the farmers paid little rent. But theirs was the best land for partridges'.

With a good stock of wild birds to look after, his main task was to keep the vermin down. 'There were lots of stoats about – I trapped thirty-five in my first week, in 1908, with the ordinary steel gin. I was paid about nine or ten bob a week; the head then had about a guinea a week and a farm worker 13s or 14s. But we also managed to nab a few cats and their skins were worth 4s each. A lot of farmers kept cats for killing rats and mice, but they didn't feed them of course, and they often got onto a partridge beat, where they did a lot of damage. Mind you, we had to be careful about killing them, and still sometimes got into trouble.'

In common with keepers on most other estates, George received one suit of clothes a year. 'Colonel Witmore used to go salmon fishing to Norway a great deal so he used to send wool over there to have cloth made up, and from this our local tailor made the suits.

'The beaters wore just ordinary clothes. Their pay was 2s 6d men and bob a day lads. There was no trouble getting beaters as long as you had plenty of beer – 7d a pint it was then, and it used to come out in big stone jars – three or four gallons each.'

In time-honoured fashion, George plotted all the partridge nests on a map of his beat, and understandably it was most dispiriting to see foxes making great inroads

George Pryke of Shropshire has been one of keepering's great survivors

into his charges. 'It was all good hunting country so we weren't supposed to shoot the devils, but we all had ways of getting round this. We usually shot the adults and fed a few cubs, which the huntsman would see and go home happy. Yes, there were plenty of tricks in those days.'

Another of his wrinkles was to ring the nests with oil of tar or animal oil to stop dogs and foxes scenting the sitting partridges which 'had a lot of heat and scent in them'.

Considering all the trouble that keepers such as George took in caring for their birds, it was sometimes very disappointing see a poor team of Guns let loose on them. For example, there was the day when the Johnson brothers (the tarmac people who rented part of the Dudmaston shooting) invited no less than fourteen business colleagues to shoot, and they were all inexperienced Guns. There was a big drive into a 6 acre (2.5ha) field of swedes, above which was a ridge of sandstone topped with trees, resulting in what George described as 'some of the best partridges you've ever seen.

'The shooting was fast and furious', said George, 'and one Gun gave me a bob to go and fetch his second cartridge bag, but it didn't do him or anyone else any good. On that drive they shot only seven and a half brace where they should have shot fifty. One Gun was honest enough to admit he didn't stand a chance, and gave me his gun to carry all day long.

'In those days none of the toffs was really liked – they were up there and you were down here' said George, raising and lowering his hand. 'But times have certainly changed for the better and now everyone mixes in together.

'The Guns used to go to one of the farms for lunch but the keepers and beaters always took their own. No one went home sober. The chauffeur was always sent to the local pub to refill the beaters' beer jars, and the Guns always had a crate of whisky – not just one bottle.'

At the end of August 1914, twenty-year-old George volunteered for the Shropshire Yeomanry. His father was called up towards the end of the war, but by then he was fifty and 'in those days', said George, 'anyone over forty-five was an old man'.

George was a despatch rider and carried many important messages on his motorbike, with strict instructions to deliver them only to a small number of specified people, irrespective of rank. First he went to Palestine, then France in 1918. 'The only compliment I ever got from an officer was "You bloody fool". I could have taken stripes in 1914, but I refused. I said I was looking after myself and no one else in this bloody war.'

When George returned from the war in January 1919 – fortunately in the first draft because he had a job to go to – he was very ill and weighed only 8st 4lb (52kg). But he soon picked up as he settled back into the routine of country life.

In 1923 he went to work for Colonel Walter Kynaston at Hardwick, near Ellesmere, Shropshire, on which estate he still lives and works. The place was very run down, the old keeper had died and there was not a trap to be seen, though the land was hunted over.

Hardwick had been in the Kynaston family since 1730 and remained chiefly a partridge shoot till the great decline of the species after World War II. It then covered about 3,000 acres (1,214ha), but has since shrunk to around 1,000 acres (405ha).

George has known the present Colonel Kynaston (son of Walter) – 'Mr John' – since he was nine. 'I taught him to fish and shoot and he's quite a good Shot now.'

Not surprisingly after this long relationship, it was with some trepidation that 'Mr John' ordered the shoot's first ever poults in 1988, for until then George had reared pheasants using broody hens, the traditional method. But then this has never been a large shoot, and is still a purely family concern with just four days plus a keeper's day each season.

In earlier years George used to catch-up pheasants and later bought eggs to place under broodies. Nowadays, however, 'hens are hard to come by – in the old days they were just 2s 6d each, but do you know, in 1987 I had to pay £3 for one!' But you have to remember that George can recall when a good tip was 2s 6d and a £1 was something to talk about in the pub.

He also remembers when his favourite Gold Block tobacco was just 11d for a 2oz (50g) tin. Now it costs £2.94p 'but I only smoke 4oz a week. I've smoked since I was nine, and for many years it was fifty cigarettes a day before I changed to the pipe.

'But keepers were never what you would call poor. You could always shoot a rabbit and when I was a boy, for just half-a-crown you could buy a lump of meat big enough to feed a hungry family.'

Not surprisingly for an ex-despatch rider and a man who rode big motorbikes for most of his life, George's earliest memory concerns the roads. 'All they were was just rough Jew stones* rolled into sand. And you couldn't go anywhere without a puncture, if you were lucky enough to have tyres.'

But the man who devoted his life to sport – he can even remember shooting live pigeons from traps before it was outlawed – has no son to whom he can pass on his great store of knowledge. His wife Elizabeth died in 1969 after forty-three years of marriage, and now his only companion is his dog Rumbo, 'given to me by Jimmy McAlpine, who used to shoot here a lot and named most of his dogs after drinks'.

Even in his nineties, George still has that special walk which distinguishes the old partridge keeper, conscientiously stooping along every hedgerow, carefully marking and observing every nest. What a familiar sight he must have been in the pre-war patchwork-quilt countryside of Shropshire, and I wonder how many miles of tarred string he used to protect his partridge nests over so many years. Nor did he use any old bits of paper attached to the string: 'It had to be *The Field* as none of the other magazines or papers were strong enough!'

Apparently there was a gamekeeper who was still working when he was 100 years old, but this was in 1924; in recent times George Pryke is the oldest working keeper of whom I am aware. If any reader knows a working keeper of even greater years, do send details via the publishers, for future interest.

Note: George Pryke died peacefully on 21 January, 1994, just one month after celebrating his 100th birthday, when he was still working as a full-time gamekeeper.

* A local name for hard unmanageable rocks

STANLEY WARE
Castle Howard, Yorkshire

In the 1980s, independent television made its blockbusting series 'Brideshead Revisited' at Castle Howard, and the headkeeper then had to help keep adoring spectators off estate roads so that filming could continue. But at least the commotion did not appear to affect the pheasants, so Lord Howard, ironically Chairman of the BBC, could continue with his celebrated sport.

Castle Howard's rise to *shooting* prominence was largely due to the loyalty and skill of this one man: headkeeper Stanley Ware, who has spent most of his working life nurturing the gamebirds of Yorkshire.

Stanley was born on 5 May 1918 in the tiny village of Gillamoor near Kirbymoorside, Yorkshire. His father was a rabbit catcher for much of the year, mostly September to April; otherwise he would break up stones in the quarries and dig trenches for water pipes at 3d a yard.

Most of the rabbits were ferreted or caught in gin traps and snares; only a few were shot because a couple of good, 'clean' rabbits would fetch 1/6d whereas a couple of shot ones made only between 8d and 10d. 'But father didn't get all that', said Stanley. 'He was employed by Colonel Holt and his estate paid him 3d for each rabbit caught. Most rabbits were crated and put on the train for the London markets. But there were a lot of rabbits then and a lot people were worse off than us. And in the Great War, when father was rejected by the Army on account of his feet, the Government sent him all over the place to keep the rabbits down on many estates.'

When he was still at school at Gillamoor, Stanley started to become interested in keepering through his grandfather, who was a beatkeeper for Lord Feversham at Nawton Towers. But Stanley had to walk the eight miles to visit him.

At the age of twelve, Stanley had his first experience as a beater, for Colonel Holt on the Ravenswick estate, near Kirbymoorside. The pay was 2s a day, but beaters had to take their own lunch and cold tea in a bottle as there were no flasks in those days. Very often Stanley was given one of the easy jobs as a stop because he knew the ground well through going there with his father to catch rabbits.

Stanley was pleased to leave school at the age of fourteen, to get out into the fresh air and help his father with his work. He did not have to set the ginns because he was particularly good at snaring – 'The best place to snare was where the rabbits ran across a grass field to feed in a field of roots. It was quite easy to spot their runs in the long grass, especially after frost.' In return for this work, Stanley received free board and lodging with his parents, but no pay.

Four years later the headkeeper at Castle Howard asked Stanley's father, who caught rabbits there, if he knew of a lad who wanted to take up keepering. Not surprisingly, he suggested his own son, and thus in 1936 began an association which has lasted to this day.

His employer was the late Lord Grimthorpe, who then leased about half of the Castle Howard estate and had a brood mare farm there; he was also a Master of the Middleton Foxhounds. Headkeeper was Joe Durno, 'a damn good man', and Stanley was paid about 10s a week, of which 5s went to his aunt for lodging with her at the appropriately named Gunthorpe village on Castle Howard estate.

He started at the end of February and one of his main tasks was killing vermin, especially crows, magpies, jays and jackdaws. The main method of catching crows was to place eggs on a tree stump to entice the birds down and lure them into a trap. 'But foxes were taboo. Being an MFH, Lord Grimthorpe would have sacked us if he had seen us shoot one. So generally they were left alone, and if one became a real nuisance it had to be a three o'clock in the morning job!'

In the late thirties farming was more sympathetic towards game and wildlife. There were many more hedgerows and no spraying so the partridges could usually be left to fend for themselves. The keeper's main work was concerned with rearing large numbers of pheasants, and that really got underway in April when rabbit catching was finished with. 'At home we rarely ate rabbit and mother always had to disguise it in the cooking pot. But father always knew it was there. You can hardly blame him for turning his nose up at it, having had to gut them all day long.

'Our broody hens were bought from farms and local people – everybody kept a few hens – for 2s 6d each, and put into sitting boxes with six compartments. The hen's quota of eggs depended on her size and varied from eighteen to twenty.

Before they were protected, sparrowhawks and kestrels were commonly shot by keepers, including Stanley Ware at Castle Howard

Stanley Ware and headkeeper Joe Durno at Castle Howard in the days when pheasants were reared under broody hens

'Every morning the hens were taken out of their boxes and tethered by one leg to a stick, and each hen had to be put back onto her own nest; after a few days they got used to this. When a hen was taken off the nest, the keeper had to put his hands under the bird and move her back slightly to lift her feet from the eggs so that she would not drag them forward and break them on the board. Then the hen was passed to another man, who put her on her tether.

'Before and during sitting the hens were dusted with louse powder to kill any fleas they might be carrying. Infested birds would shift about relentlessly on the eggs and break quite a few.

'During the first part of incubation the hens were allowed only a short time off the eggs, but as time went on they were allowed longer spells off duty. When they were finally put back on the eggs we went round with shovel and hose to clean up any mess they had made or food not eaten. And we always turned the drinking bowls upside down to keep vermin away.

'The siting of the sitting boxes was very important. Too much direct sun would make the hens shift about on the nest, and even sometimes rise from the eggs, which would then be chilled. They had to be placed a few inches above ground level in case of heavy rain, ideally on a ridge of sandy soil which was well drained. At the same time this made it a little bit easier for the keeper to remove the birds.

'This done, the nests were shaped with a rounded stone and lined with hay or dried grass into which hot eggs were placed. These were left with the hens for a couple of days to discover which were the best sitters. Some of the hens never took to the boxes after running around free on the farms. And we had to put a wire fence around the boxes to keep out dogs and foxes.

'While the hens were still sitting the rearing field had to be prepared, first by putting tunnel traps all around the hedgerows. Then we cut rides about a yard wide across the field to stand the coops in, twenty yards between the rows and twenty yards between each coop. All this covered several acres of land, which was rented from one of the tenant farmers.

'When the coops were first put out they were turned upside down and limewashed inside. Small runs were placed in front of the coops for the first few days. Then along came the rearing hut complete with pans, buckets and feeding bowls. And as soon as possible we had to find lots of dry wood to store under the hut in case of wet weather as all the food was boiled.

'By this time all the chicks were hatching out. When they had dried off under their broody they were taken to the rearing field in boxes, the hen in a sack. In each coop a hen had about eighteen chicks.

'Then we started boiling the food. Eggs were cooked forty at a time and put through a fine sieve. Rice, kibbled maize, linseed and wheat were boiled too. This was all mixed up in the feeding bowl with scalded fine biscuit meal and finally dried off with barley meal and dusted with a tiny amount of Pheasant-rina spice to make the food taste better.

'After each feed the bowls were immediately put into boiling water as soft food soon went sour. The coops were moved onto fresh ground every day or two.

'Often the chicks became infested with gapes: these are little, pink worms which get into the windpipe and lungs, and if they are not treated up to half the birds could die. We would block up most of the air vents in the coop and use bellows to blow in some powder call Kamlin, which the birds breathed in for a few minutes.

'At this time of year you were on the rearing field from six in the morning till the birds were shut up at night, and as the birds got older this became later: on very mild nights it could be eleven o'clock.

'With three keepers on this shoot, two were on the rearing field while the other went around the woods cutting rides with a scythe ready to receive the coops and in preparation for the birds' release.

'At four to five weeks old the birds were moved to cover. The night before they would be fastened in; we would place a sack under the coop and lift the thing bodily onto a cart, and as we had a horse to pull it we could reach wherever we wanted to go. The coops were placed out on the ride as on the rearing field, but the hens were facing in all directions so that they could give us warning when any vermin came in sight.

The rearing field hut at Castle Howard

'The hens stayed in the wood for several weeks before being taken home. By this time they were in laying condition and sold as laying hens for the same price as we gave for them.

'The keeper still had to boil the food and see the birds had plenty of water. His last job before going home for the night was to boil the food ready for the morning feed. At the same time he would see the birds had some grit and light the hurricane lamps to keep the foxes away.

'From twelve weeks old the birds started to stray away from the coverts so then we used a dog to drive them back home.

'Lord Grimthorpe was a real gent, but Colonel Deacon took charge of the shooting for him as he was away hunting several days a week. The other Guns were mostly ex-military. We had about four partridge days of 50–70 brace each and ten or so covert shoots with bags of 140–150 pheasants.

'Our beaters were paid 2s 6d a day and given a bottle of beer each. The lucky ones were given a cartridge bag to carry and for this they might get an extra half-crown each. One gentleman used to give a pound so everybody rushed for him.

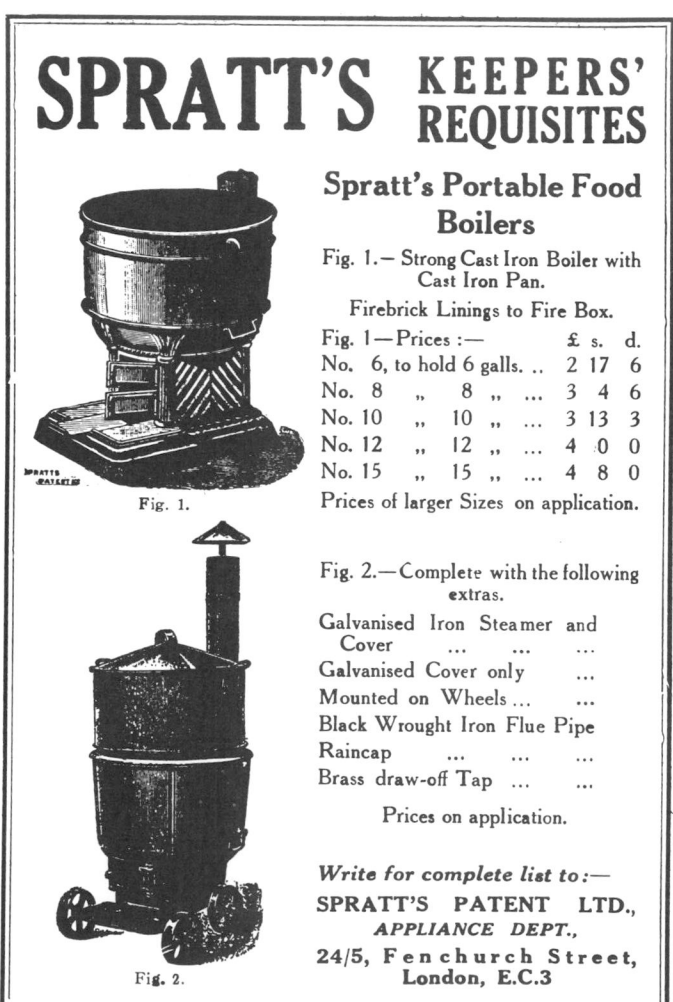

1932

Young Stanley Ware (centre) and keeper Fox (right) at Castle Howard

'The poachers then were all local people as there was very little transport. But we had to be nightwatching from the start as they could still take a lot of birds. We used to take turns with neighbouring keepers to watch for these trouble-makers – one man in the Territorial Army used to knock off birds with his .303.

'When the shooting season was over we had hen pheasants to catch for the laying pens, about seven hens to each cock. This done, we started on the rabbit population as in those days there were so many of them. After some time at them with ginns, snares, ferrets and guns, a lot of them would take to sitting out on top. These were dealt with by a few farm tenants and others who helped during the nesting season. The keeper drove the rabbits forward with dogs and hopefully they were shot by the people standing forward. But we still left snares and traps going until April.

'Then we started on carrion crows and magpies, which were sitting by this time. Tunnel traps were kept going for ground vermin.

'Early pheasants started to lay in April and English partridges early in May. We found as many of these as possible so we could put Renardine around the nests in cartridge cases to take away the scent of the birds, which otherwise might attract predators. On wet days we went to the shed to creosote the coops and sitting boxes.

'By the middle of May it was time to start all over again with the broody hens.'

This regime continued until January 1940 when Stanley was called up to join the Royal Artillery; he hoped to 'give 'em what for from a long distance. At first I was stationed all over England, but in March 1942 I was sent to Ceylon and then to India for three or four years.'

The worst incident Stanley saw in service was at the Filton aircraft factory near Bristol when he was on ack-ack defence. 'We couldn't reach the bombers with those peashooters and one Wednesday they dropped a stick of bombs right across the countryside because they were not sure where the factory was. One fell directly onto an air-raid shelter and killed a hundred people.

'Next day our boys sent in a squadron of Hurricanes. Jerry came again on Friday, our lads took off and we thought that's the last we'll see of them. Then suddenly they reappeared out of the cloud, came right down on Jerry and knocked out eleven bombers in as many minutes.'

After the war Lord Grimthorpe lost his lease at Castle Howard so Stanley worked single-handed for three doctors on another part of the estate, having been highly recommended by both Durno and Deacon. Part of the land encompassed Stanley's old beat so he knew the ground well. Rowntrees of York boss Dickinson ran the shoot on behalf of the medical men – a gynaecologist, a GP and a radiologist – and started Stanley on £2 a week, but he did also get a good income from the sale of rabbits.

Boxing Day was 'the big one', when wives and families always turned out to beat 'and I had a job to keep 'em all in line. And it was a good job I had a few Christmas boxes, as tips were few then. The most you would ever receive was £1 but I would say I never really had a good tip in my life. They don't realise what a keeper has to do to put a few shots over them.'

During his eighteen years with the doctors, Stanley lived in a rented house at nearby Welburn, having married during the war.

Then came a telephone call from Mr (later Lord) George Howard of Castle Howard, asking him to go for interview with a view to replacing the headkeeper Joe Durno, who had unexpectedly taken a job as a milkman at Malton. Stanley was the obvious choice as he had been on the estate the longest.

Mr Howard interviewed Stanley in his office at the Castle in January 1964, prior to starting the job in February – traditionally the beginning of the keepering year. Stanley told him he had been on the estate since 1936. 'Good Lord', said Mr Howard, 'and I hardly know you'. The truth was that he had never even spoken to Stanley before. In fact he hardly ever spoke to anyone on a shoot day and, in Stanley's words, 'could be rather odd at times. He was a fairly good shot with his Purdeys and loader, but he was away from home a lot with his BBC commitments (a governor from 1972 and Chairman 1980–83) and everything to do with the shooting parties had to be organised for him by his wife, Lady Cecilia, the daughter of the Duke of Grafton. When he came home at the weekend all he had to do was pick up a gun.'

Stanley started on £12 a week in 1964, payable fortnightly in arrears, but there was also a dog allowance of 10s a week and the cottage was rent and rates free. He had the help of five other keepers as the idea was to build the shoot up; Mr Howard had started to take land back, at the same time injecting a considerable amount of cash. Thus bags rose from around 120 in 1964 to over 400, Stanley's highest being 700 for one day.

Stanley Ware outside his Castle Howard cottage in 1988, with his old anti-poacher truncheon

There has been a steady stream of interesting guests on the mostly two-day shoots. Lord Whitelaw has been a regular – 'a grand chap, not an outstanding Shot but he killed a hundred birds here one day and he was very pleased with that. Anglia Television chairman Lord Buxton, the *Survival* wildlife film maker and conservationist, has been quite a bit, too.'

But like all headkeepers, Stanley did not actually see much of the Guns on shoot days: he was too busy organising his retinue. 'Sometimes I did not see them at all until after the last drive. One of my biggest problems was getting 'em back out after lunch at the Castle. This usually went on from about 1 to 2.30pm or 2.45pm, and of course, there wasn't much light left then in December – perhaps time for only one short drive. And you hadn't to strike a match when you passed those merry Guns! It was entirely Lord Howard's fault.'

Yet Stanley obviously had great respect for his master. 'Lord Howard once shot a pheasant which fell through the ice on a pond near the house. A keeper's spaniel was sent to retrieve it, but fell through and couldn't get out. Without hesitation, Lord Howard plunged into the icy water up to his neck, with stick in hand to smash his way through to the struggling dog.

'Eventually he succeeded and the dog scrambled out, but it took about seven of us to free Lord Howard as it was very muddy and he was a very big chap.

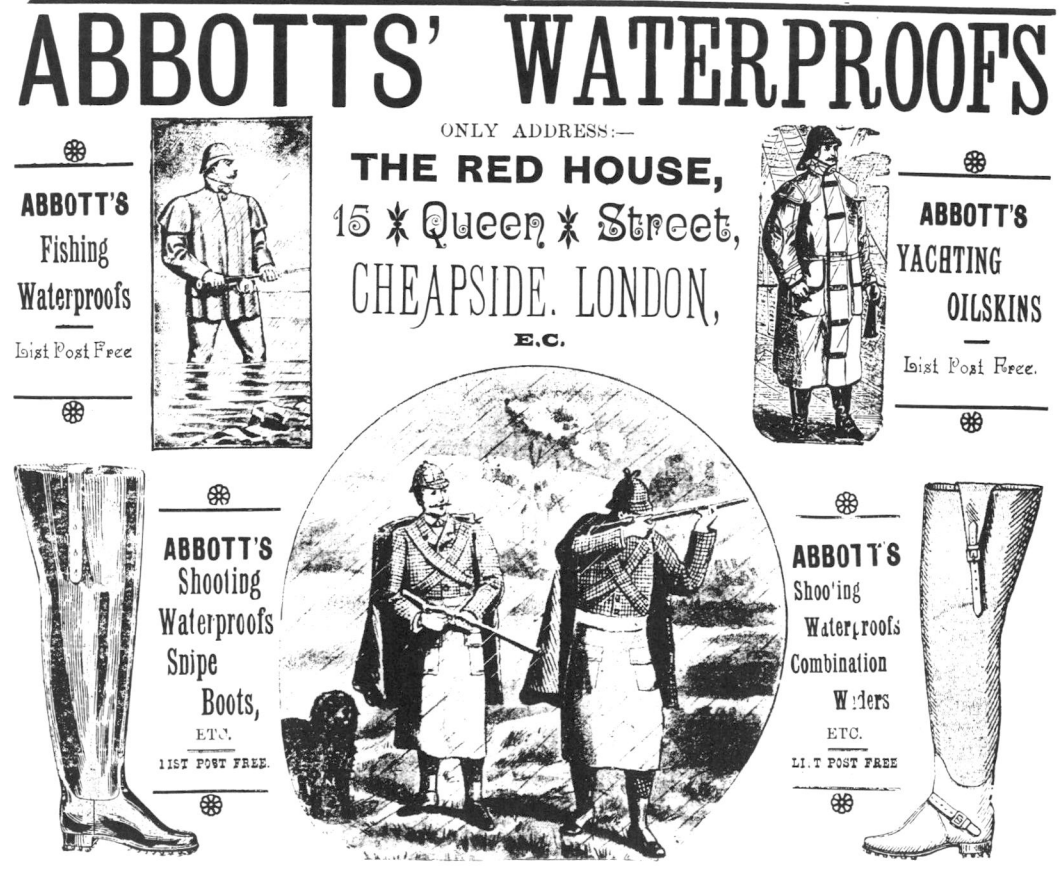

1895

Stanley Ware (centre, sitting) received his long-service award at the 1988 CLA Game Fair at Floors Castle. Also pictured are the other award-winning keepers (front), the Duke of Roxburghe (centre, standing) and the Duke of Atholl (standing, third from left)

'It was a wonderful effort on his behalf and I decided to write to the RSPCA about it as I thought they should give him one of their awards. But do you know they threw it out because it happened on a shoot day, despite the fact it certainly saved the dog's life. I was furious, and when I told her ladyship about it she said: "Well, I've patronised the RSPCA for years, but I'm afraid this will have to be the end of it."'

Lady Cecilia was involved in another shooting incident which remains clear in Stanley's mind, though she never used a gun herself. 'We were driving partridges, hares and rabbits with the tenant farmers and there were three Guns each side of a fence when we came to a potentially dangerous spot where I had placed a blue plastic bag in the fence, to warn people *not* to shoot towards it.

'At the end of the drive a hare came forward and one of the Guns swung through it and towards the bag. I cried out "No, No", but he still fired and immediately there was a yell from the other side. The silly . . . had put a few pellets into the legs of both another Gun and her ladyship, who was standing with him.

'We used to have up to fifty volunteers on hare shoots as the agent used to write to the tenant farmers saying "Bring a friend". I never knew who would turn up and many of them would be very inexperienced.'

Another guest from the world of television was one-time BBC director-general Alisdair Milne, who certainly made an impression on Stanley, but for all the wrong reasons. 'Judging by what he left me at night, I don't think he was a shooting man: he never left me a penny!'

The 'undesirables' also included the then boss of the Comet discount shops, Mr Hollingbury. 'His syndicate bought five days one year and eight the next and he complained about everything. On his last day we guaranteed a bag of 200 and they shot 232, yet he still moaned to me. When I told Lord Howard he said: "Right, he's out". Mind you, Hollingbury didn't winge when we shot 400!'

Stanley has worked on the estate under five agents, one of whom was Lord Morpeth (now Viscount Morpeth). But when Lord Howard became ill, and since his death, the third of his four sons, the Honourable Simon, took over the running of the estate – but there is no lord of the manor now, as Simon's father had been a life peer.

Many of the traditions continue, even though most shoot days are sold now. They still hold a Christmas party at the Castle for all the staff and everyone receives a present – in the old days only the heads of staff were invited. 'Young' Simon Howard still takes Stanley a brace of pheasants at Christmas – though the keeper admits to not liking pheasant too much and prefers it cold.

Stanley retired from full-time keepering in 1983, but did a further three years part-time. He received his CLA long-service award for forty-seven years in 1988, and now lives in a delightful divided cottage on the estate, where he and his wife tend a very traditional garden bursting with flowers and magnificent vegetables. But he stresses that 'the pheasant is not the gardener's friend', and he now views them differently as they parade along his wall.

Mrs Gertrude Ware is an excellent cook ('she was my underkeeper, you know – strong as I was'), but a low-sugar diet means that she has to resist most of the fine fare she puts on for Stanley. Despite their remoteness, they are well served by visiting traders – the butcher, fishmonger and baker all still call regularly, a luxury rare in much of England today.

Typically Spartan, but interesting with its mementoes of old country life, the Ware cottage is extremely quiet – when I was there the only sounds were the tick of the clock and, appropriately, the occasional *kok-kok* of a pheasant. It is indeed a fitting place in which to recall the highlights of a successful partnership. For Mrs Ware there is the cherished memory of being given a small role, along with other locals, when Paul Newman, Sophia Loren and David Niven came to film at Castle Howard; and for Stanley there is immense pride in a lifetime devoted to sporting duty, throughout which 'everyone called me Stan – even his lordship'.

Jack Clark
Sandringham

When Jack Clark marched behind the coffin of George VI along with the other Sandringham keepers there were tears in his eyes, for he had seen the passing not only of a great Shot but also of a man devoted to shooting and all its followers. Jack's father was also in that procession from Sandringham Church to Wolferton Station in 1952, marking a long family commitment to the royal family.

'George VI really liked duck shooting and rabbit shooting best', Jack told me at his very attractive Victorian retirement cottage at West Newton on the Sandringham estate. 'We often had to walk the woods for him in between main shooting days, so we was never done. But he had to slacken up in the last few years when he became ill.

'I spoke to him on the hare shoot the day before he died: he said goodnight to us and we said goodnight to him. Everything seemed much the same as usual.

'Next day we was pushin' a load of rabbits home on a bike when we met the farm foreman. He said "I suppose you know the news". "No" we all chirruped together. And with a lump in his throat he said "The King's dead. Old Jimmy McDonald the valet found him when he took up his cup of tea"'.

Christened John Edward, Jack Clark was born on 29 April 1923 at Great Wilbraham, Cambridgeshire, where his father and his grandfather before him had been keeper for Squire Hicks.

In 1934 the family moved to Sandringham, when Jack's father, Nobby, became beat keeper at Flitcham. And after schooling at Flitcham and West Newton, fourteen-year-old Jack not surprisingly started work in 1937 on the Wolferton beat, where he was to remain for the whole of his working life, apart from war service. 'In those days there were very few job opportunities so you took what you could. I might have gone in the Army, but you had to take a test and I weren't too good at arithmetic'.

For a month or two before starting on pheasant work Jack worked as houseboy for the retired schoolmaster who looked after the King's racing pigeons. 'When the old boy died the lofts were closed.'

Working under his father, Jack did a lot of vermin trapping and, as 'the junior', he was heavily involved in the routine feeding programme which included the usual mix of eggs, rice, scalded biscuit meal and 'hundreds and hundreds of minced, boiled rabbits. We fed three or four times a day and the food stove never went out, even if it was pissin' with rain.

'All the coops were kept in a great big shed and for days on end we had to scrub them out with Jeyes Fluid, and then they were limewashed. And all the runs had to be creosoted.

The Sandringham gamekeepers marching behind George VI's coffin from Sandringham Church to Wolferton Station in 1952. Jack Clark is pictured second from the left in the second row and his father is front right

'Each clutch was made up to about twenty eggs and it was very important that the broods were kept separated. So we put each chick in a little marked bag to make sure they all ended up with the right hens after being crated to the rearing field about a mile away – the hens would brain the wrong chicks.

'Each coop contained a faggot of rhododendron for the chicks to hide in till the grass got high, and we moved the coops every day. The chicks demanded a great deal of attention so we used to pray for a cold night so that we could shut them up early and not have to watch them.

'Days were specially long if there was big vermin trouble and we sometimes had to stay in the cabins all night. And you know what it's like working for father. Not only did he make me gather all the firewood in a pony and cart, but I had to take him his dinner on me bike, too!

'We were on the rearing field for six to eight weeks as there were two hatches. When the first lot went to wood it was often two weeks before the others would be off. One of our biggest problems was that if they was sick there were no drugs to dose the birds up: all we could do was shift 'em to fresh ground and hope they would get better.'

Rearing stopped at Sandringham with the outbreak of war and there has been none since, though a few pheasants were reared in 1940 on another beat.

When the war started in September 1939 Jack's father immediately joined the Army. In fact Nobby had a distinguished military career. After 12 months he was selected to train Special Operations Executive agents – such as Odette Churchill – in survival techniques, and was eventually commissioned. He had also been mentioned in despatches in 1919 during the Afghan War: Jack still has the framed citation signed by Winston Churchill, who was then Secretary of State for War (And Air).

At Sandringham, some of the best seasons' bags were commemorated in special colour paintings by Lady Fellowes, wife of ex Sandringham agent Sir William Fellowes

Jack joined up at the end of 1941, serving with the Norfolks (his father's regiment) in North Africa, Italy and Europe, the Sherwood Foresters (with whom he was wounded in Italy), and the King's Shropshire Light Infantry. He returned home in 1946.

Shooting had continued at Sandringham during the war, when there were some good partridge years – about 6,000 were shot one season. 'With the let-down of the war, wild pheasants and partridges found ideal conditions here and really came into their own. There was no going back to the old days of heavy rearing, when they thought nothing of shooting 2,000 pheasants or 300–400 brace of partridges on a single outing. The total number shot must have been enormous and we always wondered how accurate the gamebooks were. Large quantities were sent off to market and we always reckoned that somebody must have made a fortune.

'In those days neighbouring estates too were taken for the shooting, but that all finished with Edward VIII. On some beats, if they didn't kill more than 2,000 the first time over then someone was for the high jump. Anmer was probably the best beat. But I was only a lad then.

'Father had a lighter suit for partridge shooting, which often took place in fine weather early in the season, but for pheasant days he wore a big, dark-green

beatkeeper's coat, cord breeches, gaiters and a hard bowler hat with a gold braid sash and two acorns around. It was ever such a heavy coat – what it would cost today goodness only knows.'

Before the war the beaters wore blue, numbered smocks, 'and there were two gangs of them on partridge days as there was no transport to whizz people around in. In fact there were still two gangs for a while after the war.'

In those days the keeper's lunch consisted of 'a great chunk of bread – about half a cottage loaf, cheese, meat, beer and mince pies – all wrapped up in a little parcel. The Guns had a special marquee for lunch, and headkeeper Bland had his own little tent adjoining it. Mother did out our big front room for the loaders of the guests, but we used to be all right for grub for about a fortnight afterwards, what with sauces, cold meats, pickles, chutneys and suchlike.

'Headkeeper Bland was not a popular man. He looked just like George V and rode about on a pony checking up on everybody. All the keepers had to call him "Sir" – you wouldn't have dared address him by his Christian name in those days.'

Like other headkeepers of the period, Bland made spot checks on the partridge nests marked on each beatkeeper's map, looking at perhaps three or four hundred nests on one beat as often as he could. 'There were so many birds here then. Why, on my mile and a half walk to school I could spot about thirty partridge nests in the hedgerow, but today you would be lucky to see half-a-dozen. Of course, you spotted the most in a good nestin' year and when the growth didn't come too soon.'

As a junior, Jack's other jobs included 'putting out hundreds of yards of sewelling to stop birds breaking back, and taking out lunches to as many as twenty "stops". The stops were mostly older men who found it hard to keep up with the line, but some poor devils had to stay put all day, gently tapping to stop the birds running out the sides.'

At first Jack earned 'Ten or twelve bob a week', but after paying his keep ended up with 'only about two bob pocket money', so he was much better off in the Army, when he had the whole of his ten bob pay to spend.

No doubt his Army experience helped prepare him for the inevitable occasional brush with poachers. Jack's worst experience was in 1955, when he came across a gang of three at night. 'I fetched one bloke down but the other buggers came back at me. I was on the ground when I saw the raised gun and instinctively put my hand up to defend myself. I'm sure that saved me from having a clobbered skull, but the rifle butt did smash several ribs.

'But I had my own back once or twice. Father did too. Take the time when he struggled with a man holding a .410 and the gun went off right next to his head when he was holding it by the muzzle. The man got away, but next day they found the gun's fore-end along with a box of matches at the scene of the incident.

'The following Sunday a gang of five from Wisbech were seen poaching on another part of the estate and were picked up by the police. Next morning the police inspector found that one of the gang's guns matched the fore-end found the week before. The police knew one of the gang well – a seventeen-year-old – so put the heat on him and he coughed the lot. Just before the war that was.'

As Jack told me this story in his pretty little cottage, swifts continually swooped past the windows. 'How lucky you are', I remarked, but Mrs Clark interjected 'I

Even in retirement, Jack Clark of Sandringham remains closely attached to his dogs

don't like 'em bombing my washing line though'. 'You should like birds, dear', said Jack quietly, but firmly.

A bachelor most of his life, Jack married in 1980 – quite a change for the man who, prior to retirement in April 1988, lived for fifty years in the same cottage in Wolferton woods, where he still does a little vermin control. He gets 'a decent pension' from the estate, 'and there was a lump sum on retirement', but now he has to pay part of the rent, whereas once it was entirely free.

The cottage is crammed with photos and other reminders of the shooting life. Included among the treasures are Jack's royal Victorian medal, which he received from Her Majesty the Queen in 1986, and the CLA keeper's long-service award, which he received at Chatsworth in 1987. 'It was for forty years, but actually I had done forty-nine then.'

But the objects of yesteryear mean no more than the memories – clearly stretching back to the day when George V handed Jack an orange on a visit to the local school. 'I never saw him shoot, but I understand he was a pretty good Shot.

'The Duke of Edinburgh and Prince Charles are excellent Shots, though Charles doesn't do much shooting now and Philip gets bad arthritis in his hands: you always know when it's playing him up on a cold day because he misses more than usual and then swears a lot. Lord Brabourne is perhaps the best Shot I've seen, though he can be a bit greedy. Today I would say that the three best regular Shots at Sandringham are Hugh van Cutsem, Anthony Duckworth-Chad of Pinkney Hall, Norfolk and Lord Tollemache of Helmingham Hall, Suffolk. Prince Edward is not a particularly good Shot.

'Most shooting at Sandringham takes place in January now. The Queen never shoots, but what a keen gundog lady she is. All the dogs love her and make a great fuss of her. She had handled my old bitch Pendle and now whenever the dog sees Her Majesty she will make straight for her – even if she is a hundred yards away. All she wants is a bit of fuss made of her and then she comes straight back to me.

'Overall, it's been a good life, but I've certainly had some hassle. I'm the sort of bloke who worries and would have been no good as a headkeeper. I don't know if I'd do it all over again. I missed the Army you know, especially when I was demobbed. When you came back to a little ol' bloody village like Wolferton after years abroad nobody knew you, and you couldn't join up with the regulars if you were all crocked up like I was with my injuries.'

The Ideal Gamekeeper

He must be imbued with an iron constitution, able to withstand all weathers, do without sleep whenever necessary and be able to snatch a few moments in the lee of a hedge or haystack, to be of a build able to hold his own against odds, and also to be tactful when required.

He must have a real love for the life, a past master of woodcraft, and find a pleasure in attending to the many small duties which go to make a successful whole. He must be anxious to study the ways and habits of all wild nature and to be able to read from their movements and calls what is transpiring in their vicinity.

To be able, when going his rounds, to know by the signs whether game has been netted, killed by vermin, or shot; if traps or snares are or have been set in rabbit burrows and runs, or long nets set along a wood side; able to note any broken branches in a wood, and find out the cause. Footprints of all kinds should be an open book to him.

There is no reason for him to be unsociable, but it is best not to make it a habit of going into company, particularly public assemblies, for once it is seen that he has a propensity to this, someone is sure to take advantage of it.

When in due course he is offered the post of headkeeper it will be wise on his part to go slowly on entering this position and not to be too arrogant to his assistants. They have perhaps been some years on the estate and are conversant with its peculiarities, and he will do well to get their opinions without showing as far as possible that he is asking for information, and in this way he may learn a lot about the estate which otherwise time only would have shown.

J. Parker, 1931

Killer Poachers

Vicious attacks on gamekeepers were very common in former times and it seems that poachers were more ready to use their guns in anger than is the case nowadays. The following article is from *Shooting Times*, 6 May 1887:

Very early on Thursday, William Illingworth and Edward Copley, the head and second keepers on the Badsworth Hall estate, near Pontefract, belonging to Mr R. B. H. Jones, were out watching on Badsworth Common, near to Royd Moor. While upon Mr Nicholson's farm they spied two poachers, each armed with a gun; and they eventually came close upon them in a wheat field near the embankment of the Swinton and Knottingley Railway. Illingworth, a hale man of about 50 years of age, instantly ordered the poachers to stand, and struck the elder of the two men a heavy blow across the head. The headkeeper's stick was broken by the force of the blow, and he thereupon called to Copley for assistance. The latter stepped forward to obey the command of his superior, but his endeavours were quickly frustrated. One of the poachers, without any ado, shouldered his gun, and, while only a couple of yards distant, emptied the charge of his piece into Copley's left side. Copley was brought to the ground, and Illingworth was left to the mercy of the two assailants. They beat him severely about the head, and in order to escape extreme peril, he feigned

Poacher and lurcher – a constant threat

unconsciousness, hoping thereby to persuade the men that they had done their worst at him. The poachers then made off.

With a view to meeting the worst, Copley's depositions were taken, and the precaution proved a wise one, as the unfortunate man died on Saturday evening. As yet, neither of the poachers has been caught, although their arrest is regarded as certain, both being known to the police. The murder of police-constable Austwick by the notorious Murphy, and the shooting of Thirkill, Lord Wharncliffe's gamekeeper, in 1867, render the district in which the outrage occurred notorious. The suspected men in the present case are Cudworth colliers, who are supposed to be in hiding near Normanton. As we go to press, we hear that the suspected men are named Pilmore and Roberts, that the coroner's inquest resulted in a verdict of wilful murder against them, and that a warrant has been issued for their apprehension.

A few weeks later a reader wrote to the editor of *Shooting Times* with the following comment:

I do not agree with those who think the keeper Illingworth acted well. It is not wise to rush up to people who have loaded guns in their hands and break sticks over their heads. To successfully encounter poachers armed with guns requires plenty of smartness, not ill-mannered brusqueness. As a rule, keepers and policemen are the most uncouth, ill-mannered men in creation. If they are such fools to risk their lives over a fifteenpenny rabbit, all I can say is the same as you say when a poor man gets in jail for a bit of rabbiting: 'Serve them jolly well right'. The game is not worth the candle.

Hedgehogs for Rheumatism

When gamekeeper Joseph Williams apprehended gypsy William Pool in 1887, the nomad said he was 'searching for hedgehogs, from which he extracted oil for the benefit of his rheumatism'. Little wonder that Willenhall Police Court did not believe him, especially as he and an accomplice had a ferret and a dog with them on the land of Mr J. L. Vernon at Hilton Park. Charged with trespassing in pursuit of game, Pool was fined 5s and costs, together with 1s for the damage to a fence, making in all £1 14s 6d. In default of payment he would be sentenced to one month's hard labour.

The egg thief

Night watch

'Night' Eyes

I do not believe that any man possesses keener 'night' eyes than the average gamekeeper, the only other individual approaching him in this particular being the rural police constable, who is also accustomed to patrolling the darkness. Nevertheless, the latter paces along roads and footpaths, and has little need to penetrate rough fields and coverts, and, had he to do so, would probably soon be at fault. Once, in a police court I listened to a dispute between rival solicitors as to whether a keeper could possibly have identified a man accused of poaching at night, under the conditions of darkness described. Possibly you and I could not have done so, but the gamekeeper stands in a different category as regards seeing at night. On several occasions I have been flight shooting at night with keepers, and in each instance been astonished at their success, which far exceeded mine and was entirely attributable to the possession of better sight. I must say that the keeper is generally closely acquainted with the surface of the ground he has to cover at night, having so often traversed it during broad daylight, but he is just as clever in strange country.

Midnight marauder

The keeper is not enamoured of carrying a lantern whatever the duty he has to undertake at night, even the policeman's bullseye not being in favour with him. For one purpose only does he regularly take advantage of artificial light and that is for stopping fox earths in preparation for hunting. It is necessary that an earth should be surely closed, for the presence of the smallest gap will tempt a fox to tear a passage in. The keeper was one of the first to realise the possibilities of the electric torch, and when this was placed on the market it was not long before every keeper possessed one. What he had looked for all his life was a light he could call into action at any moment, to recognise an intruder, or ascertain the safety of the next step. The torch provided for all this, without inflicting on the person carrying it bulk and weight.

A further duty of the keeper for which a light is absolutely necessary is for attending to his rabbit traps at night. He might be able to remove rabbits caught without the help of a light, but if his trapping is to meet with full success traps must be re-set, and that is a risky undertaking when it is dark. An ordinary lantern, lit by a candle, affords but a poor, flickering light, and this is not easily directed onto the actual spot where one is required to work. The lantern was continually being knocked over, and the candle wasted by guttering. An oil lamp was better, but if

52

burning petroleum, tainted the surroundings, and interfered with the success of the trapping. The electric torch has done much to reduce the cruelty of trapping, it being so perfect for the trapper's use that he is encouraged to visit his traps before retiring to rest. If the torch is fixed to a short peg this may be inserted in the ground and the ray of light directed just where required. When not needed the light may be snapped off, and does not advertise the presence of the keeper.

'Hoverer' 1941

Wartime Dog Diet

With food rationing, the difficulties of keeping a large kennel were only too obvious during World War II and keepers had enough trouble maintaining a balanced diet for even one animal. But as usual our sportsmen showed great initiative and this generated considerable correspondence in the shooting press.

In April 1941, regular contributor Dugald Macintyre wrote about the subject in his 'Scottish Notes' for *Shooting Times and British Sportsman*: 'Having tried potatoes and greaves as dog feeding I am afraid I cannot recommend them. Dogs digest potatoes very badly, if at all, and the kennels are always in a mess where the tubers are in too liberal use. Skimmed greaves, with a little potatoes, and any sort of porridge to make bulk, makes a passable meal.

'I fancy that we might make more use of fish offal as food for dogs, but it must never be forgotten that rotten fish is absolutely poisonous for dogs as well as for people, and that bad meat seldom kills either. I suppose this war will kill the basking-shark oil-making factories. That is a pity, as we need whale-oil more than ever now, and a sharking launch might gun something else than a shark at times. Shark nets too might occasionally catch submarines, and as basking sharks are clean feeders, what about their flesh for humans as well as dogs?'

A good friend

The Cheating Hotel

When part-time keeper Patrick Fletcher called into the Three Horseshoes at Chapmanslade, Wiltshire a few years ago, he deposited about thirty dead crows in the porch, for he had been doing a spot of pest control for a local farmer. A few minutes later, as he was supping his Sunday lunchtime pint, in walked a Londoner with City pinstripe suit. The stranger asked what the crows were for and Patrick, being somewhat cagey at first, muttered something about decoys.

Then the Londoner asked if the crows were for sale. Patrick, ever concerned about the rising price of cartridges, casually asked what sort of price was being offered, and great was his surprise when the enormous sum of £2 per head was suggested. And it was cash in hand, there and then.

Hardly believing his luck, Patrick agreed, the notes were thrust into his hand and the two men enjoyed a drink together. But before the visitor departed Patrick could not resist asking him why he was willing to pay so much for mere crows. The reason was that the stranger was the manager of a leading London hotel, but before that he had been a chef. He said that the birds would be plucked and dressed and served as grouse. They had done it in the past and not one 'posh' customer would know the difference – even if someone did 'smell a rat' he would almost certainly be too polite or too embarrassed to say anything.

A crow could never be tolerated

The Sham or Pot Egg

It is not at all fully recognised how valuable these artificial eggs are on both large and small shoots, and they are made to represent the eggs of both pheasant and partridge so closely that feathered vermin are deceived and carry them off. There is nothing so efficacious in keeping both pheasants and partridges at home as these eggs, for the birds are never so prone to wander as when in search of a suitable nesting site. The sight of an artificial egg reposing in an artificial nest causes either bird at once to decide to adopt it, and if the reader is sufficiently careful to form the nests in safe places losses will be very much reduced from every cause. However a nest containing an artificial egg is concealed, it appears to be discovered by birds during their search, and, if the reader prefers that they should be more open, he may add material to hide each to a greater extent when it has been adopted. Remove the artificial egg immediately the nest has been laid in.

Shooting Times and British Sportsman, 1924

Waiting his chance

More Than He Bargained For

Middle-aged gamekeeper Edward Green, of Adisham, was admitted to the Kent and Canterbury Hospital in 1884 suffering from 'a shocking accident'. In order to destroy a wasps' nest, he filled the entrance to the hole with gunpowder and lit a slow match. The explosion happened quicker than he anticipated and blew both his hands off.

Murder of an Informer

One of four men awaiting trial in Galway Gaol, accused of murdering gamekeeper William Mahon of Ballinasloe in October 1879, decided to turn informer. Mahon was keeper to John Ross, whose Weston House was blown up with dynamite in March 1882, for which some of those concerned in the crime were sent to penal servitude. It was alleged that Mahon's refusal to join the conspiracy, and the suspicion that he was giving information, led to his doom being decreed by the local assassination society. For six months he was missing, and then his body was found in the river, sunk and tied up in a sack.

Gladstone's Finger

Evan Jones was eighty-one and a retired underkeeper; shortly before he died, at Broughton in 1895, he recalled the day Mr Gladstone lost a finger through a shooting accident. It had happened fifty-one years beforehand, at a shooting party in Hope parish, when there was an explosion as he reloaded the second barrel of his gun. Mr Gladstone's forefinger was badly torn, and on his return to Hawarden the late Dr Harrison of Chester amputated the finger in the ante-room at the rectory. Mr Gladstone's friend Sir Robert Phillimore was present and kindly assisted by holding the politician's hand. Apparently Gladstone felt little till the severe pain of the operation.

Signs of the Times

In the old days keepers were often thwarted by crafty poachers who knew that if a notice board was seen warning trespassers to keep away, then it was fairly certain that no one was on watch. Even when a lengthy list of penalties was displayed, the intruders took little notice – such warnings simply invoked ridicule and mud-slinging to deface the lettering.

Yet many people were mistaken in the belief that they were *never* watched, for keepers were often prepared to let harmless folk, such as flower-pickers, go their way unchallenged. A true brigand would have been instantly pounced upon.

Today, with far fewer men on the land, notices have become more commonplace and are more likely to receive a charge of buckshot than a harmless mud-pie.

Rabbit Petticoats

Sergeant Evans and two other police officers of the Denbigh area were out early on the Plas Chambres road on 15 September 1887 when they saw two well-known poachers, Wynne and Gallimore, coming off the land. They searched them but found nothing.

Thinking it strange that two such notorious poachers should be minus spoils, they watched and discovered that another poacher was in hiding, evidently watching the booty.

After some delay three women belonging to the men were seen going to a certain spot in an adjacent field, and after concealing something on their persons departed. On being secured by the police, twenty-seven rabbits and two big nets were found on them. The women had tied the rabbits and game by the legs and slung them over stout bands which they had fixed under their dresses like dress-improvers. The police had great difficulty in making the women part with their booty, but all were prosecuted.

In reporting the incident, *Shooting Times* editor Lewis Clement recalled how his keeper once caught a gypsy woman with seven or eight rabbits under her clothes. 'He tripped her up, as if by accident, and in her fall the rabbits, of course, were exposed to our gaze. She had obtained them by running a whippet in the warren.'

Norfolk Gamekeepers

At one time there was a marked preference among game preservers for Norfolk gamekeepers, and this is not surprising when we reflect on what these men accomplish in their own country. All the same, it must be stated that conditions in that country are very favourable to game production. A keeper advertising generally proudly proclaimed the fact that he was a Norfolk man, but we seldom see this now. A friend once advertised for a keeper and stated that no Norfolk man need apply, and I inquired his reason for that stipulation. His explanation was that foxes were not respected in that country and he required a keeper who would do so and had experience of how to defeat them without the necessity of killing them. All Norfolk is not devoid of foxes and in some parts hunting is carried on, so there are keepers who must understand Reynard pretty well and are acquainted with all his wiles.

'Hoverer', 1938

Enemy number one

The Bagged Fox

A rather grotesque incident occurred in 1939 after a keeper, certain that his coverts would be drawn blank by the local hunt, procured a fox to avoid embarrassing his employer. He placed Reynard in a bag and gave it to one of his men, with instructions to position himself in a certain covert and release the fox directly hounds appeared.

Unfortunately the man was new to the place, knew nothing of hunting or hounds, and imagined he would be in danger from the pack. The field waiting outside heard strange noises emanating from the covert, which could not be associated with the music of hounds on a fox.

The man, wishing to ensure his own safety, had climbed well up a tree, taking the fox with him. When hounds came on the scene he dropped the fox, which was so badly injured it was incapable of moving. The hounds killed it at the foot of the tree, and on arrival at the spot the huntsman immediately realised what had happened and ordered the culprit to descend. Then he laid his crop about the man's shoulders, and this castigation was the source of the strange cries heard.

The Professor's 'Hare'

In the nineteenth century gamekeepers at Holkham, on the north Norfolk coast, often used to speak of the day Mr Coke invited a well-known professor to shoot. He had never had a gun in his hand before, but Mr Coke persuaded him to join the shooting party, though care was taken to place him at a corner of the covert. Later, when the rest of the party came up to him, Mr Coke said: 'Well, what sport? You have been firing pretty often.' 'Hssh!' said the professor, 'there it goes again', and he was just raising his gun to his shoulder when a man walked very quietly out from the bushes in front of him. It was one of the beaters, who had been placed there to stop the pheasants, and his leather gaiters, dimly seen through the bushes, had been mistaken for a hare by the professor. He had been firing at 'it' whenever he saw it move, and had been much surprised by its tenacity of life. But even more surprising was the fact that the man had never discovered that the professor was shooting at him!

Like Father Like Son

At the Yorkshire Winter Assize in February 1884, before Mr Justice Field, John Lowther was sentenced to death for shooting Thomas Metcalf, headkeeper to the Earl of Zetland, at Lofthouse in Cleveland. Metcalf was shot in the right knee joint and right groin, there were no less than seventy-eight gunshot wounds and a large amount of shot had gone into the poor keeper's bones; many of the wounds were lacerated. Lowther had fired at Metcalf, at the same time wounding another keeper, when he and another poacher were being chased.

The most singular circumstance connected with the murder was that exactly forty years beforehand the father of Lowther had murdered a keeper of the Marquis of Normanby, named Moffatt, in the woods of Mulgrave, near Whitby. The father was tried at the York Assizes, 1844, and sentenced to death. Exertions were made to have the sentence commuted, and it was reduced to transportation for life. Lowther was duly sent to Australia, but, attempting to escape into the bush, was shot by one of the guards in the same part of the body that he had shot the gamekeeper Moffatt.

Killed by a Horse

Earl Darnley's headkeeper, a Mr Grundy of Cobham, near Gravesend, died in June 1895 from injuries caused by a kick from his horse while removing a stone from its hoof. Mr Grundy was described as 'a thorough sportsman, who took the keenest interest in his profession' and would be 'missed by the favoured guests of Earl Darnley'.

Armchair Pheasants

An old Hampshire keeper told me about the day in 1932 when Colonel Charles Peter Berthon of The Barns, Thorne Beech, Beaulieu was summoned at Hythe Police Court, Hampshire, for trespassing in search of game at Beaulieu. 'Pheasants kept coming into the large hall at my house and damage was being caused to the furniture', said Colonel Berthon. 'In fact', he added, 'on one occasion I saw a pheasant sitting on the arm of a valuable chair. I was annoyed and shot at the bird with an airgun. I never went outside my own property with a gun.'

It was submitted on behalf of the prosecution that if a man shot game on his own property when he had no right to do so, he was trespassing, but the Bench dismissed the case.

The reluctant flyer

The keeper's hut – home from home

The Keeper's Hut

Like the shepherd, the modern keeper has no need for temporary outdoor accommodation. His comfortable cottage is but five minutes away by Land Rover and his rearing programme no longer so labour-intensive. But not so long ago the gamekeeper's hut was a common sight about the countryside. This was neatly described by 'Hoverer' of the *Shooting Times* in 1938:

Gamekeepers who rear pheasants generally have a hut of some description available, such shelter as it affords being a necessity. Sometimes it is quite an ornate affair on wheels, or a sectional building, and very often a rough construction just hammered together. In any case its purpose is served. If a stove is fitted the hut is very comfortable for those watching at night, although too much comfort is not conducive to keen watchfulness. Near the door you are certain to see a gun standing ready to hand, and in a corner a few traps. A shelf carries a book or two, and perhaps a current copy of the *Shooting Times*. If you search into the most remote corners you may discover a pack of cards or a box of dominoes, for these do not stand revealed. After the rearing, the hut is removed to some convenient spot in the coverts, and a lamp in it at night has often sent intruders scurrying off under a belief that the keeper was there. Were he there, on the watch or listening, a light would be the last thing he would show.

61

Gamekeepers in Ireland

When game preservation is once more possible or attempted in Ireland there will be one great disadvantage to face, and this is the disappearance of the very excellent keepers who formerly carried on in Ireland. These men left with sorrow in their hearts, were often the victims of intense cruelty, and they will hardly be tempted back under any circumstances. They have had enough of it, and several have confided that fact. The majority of them were either Scots or English, or descended from settlers of those nationalities. There are very few purely Irish gamekeepers, and where they do exist are not a great success, for it is utterly impossible for them to accept a detached view of things.

If Irish keepers were a success there would not have been so many Scottish and English keepers occupying the best positions on the larger estates. Neither are at their best when they first go over, but when they have lived long enough in Ireland to understand and grasp the Irish character thoroughly they prove the men for their job. It would occupy years to train another lot like them, for they generally appeared

*Clearing rides
was back-breaking work*

The woodcock never fails to excite

as assistant keepers and worked their way up, and I am afraid no others are capable of reviving game preservation in Ireland. The feeling abroad in Ireland now is 'Ireland for the Irish', and I must say that there is little inclination on this side of the Channel to deprive them of it, or to take an energetic part in Ireland's regeneration so far as game is concerned.

'Hoverer', 1924

A Puff for the Braggard

When a group of keepers went woodcock shooting in Ireland in the 1930s one of them did not meet with much success. However, at each miss he loudly called attention to feathers flying from the bird fired at, which no one but himself could see.

The following morning, when he fired his first shot, there was a report like thunder, and the air was full of feathers. The men had got hold of his gun before they started and filled the barrels with feathers! – but it was a marvel that a burst had not occurred. This was not exactly what may be described as innocent fun but was carried out in ignorance of what the result might have been.

63

The headkeeper

HARRY GRASS

Broadlands (Hampshire), Lambton Castle (Durham),
Suffolk and Wiltshire

In his position as headkeeper for the late Earl Mountbatten at Broadlands, Harry Grass acquired a reputation as one of the greatest gamekeepers this century, and the popular press christened him 'King of the Gamekeepers'. This was indeed a great tribute to a man whose family has been the most famous in the entire history of gamekeeping. At their peak, there were 103 members of the Grass family working as keepers across the land at one time; they were all descended from two brothers – of surname Grasse and said to be refugees – who came over from France in about 1750 and arrived in the town then called Brandon Ferrie.

The Grasses certainly put down healthy roots in this country, and as their reputation grew many of them became associated with some of our finest and most famous shoots – Holkham, Elveden, Euston, Luton Hoo, Welbeck, Eaton, Lambton Castle, Studley, Six Mile Bottom and Windsor. Today, however, there are fewer than half-a-dozen members of the family remaining in the profession.

Harry's grandfather, father and all five uncles were gamekeepers. His father and Uncle Harry were keepers on the Earl of Durham's Lambton Castle Estate where Harry was born, at Houghton Gate, on 4 December 1908. He started work there as kennel boy at the age of fourteen, and under headkeeper Skelton his main job was to feed and exercise the fifty to sixty labradors, spaniels and flatcoats. But before that, while still at school, he used to sit in the woods with a .410, keeping watch over his father's pheasants.

One day his father said to him : 'Look here, if you're going to be a keeper always remember one thing – what you are looking after belongs to someone else.' Today, Harry says 'Too many people help themselves. In my time, if the boss said to me "Have a pheasant" I said thank you very much, but that was that.'

Harry's starting wage was 14s a week and after the first year he was given the keeper's uniform of a frocktail coat, breeches, box-cloth leggings and a trilby, though some keepers wore bowlers then.

At first, Harry was assigned as helper to beatkeeper Jim Hawkins, whose word was law. 'And in those days you only spoke to his lordship if you were spoken to first.'

As one of a team of twelve keepers, Harry stayed at Lambton for about a year and a half. Then one day his mother received word that Mr H. Wigmore of The Hermitage, Chester-le-Street was willing to take him on as underkeeper. So away he went, into lodgings with the head groom, to gain valuable experience.

The Hermitage had a good mixed pheasant and partridge shoot, but more unusual was its 1,400-acre (566ha) rookery, shot once a year over about a fortnight. This provided excellent sport, much of it with shotguns as well as rifles, and Harry remembers how one evening they shot over a hundred rooks on the wing!

Then came another message from his mother, to say that headkeeper Thomas Scott of Lambton wanted to see him again. Henry Bell had taken that part of Lambton known as Penshaw and wanted Harry to be second keeper under Bob Colpit. Thus Harry returned to the estate of his birth to become one of a team of four, including the colourful Smoker Watson – 'so called because he was never without his pipe'. Harry was to stay at Penshaw for four years, during which time there were four big coursing meetings every year, with plenty of hares to hand.

'Thomas Scott was always very kind to me. Father and Uncle Harry were both killed in World War I and I always had the impression that father had guessed he might not come back and asked Scott to keep an eye on me. Anyway, one day he suddenly said to me: "If you want to learn your job properly then you should go down to East Anglia."'

Harry agreed and Scott eventually found him a position as one of seven beatkeepers with Lord Henniker, the eighth Baron, at Thornham Hall, Thornham Magna, near Eye, Suffolk. 'Henniker was known as "the little old man", but he was a good Shot and a well-known field trial judge. I really enjoyed my four years with him, and during that time I met and married Stella Mayes of Thornham Magna.

'At Henniker's each man was responsible for 100–150 coops. I had to walk a mile to the rearing field and be there by 6am. We had to mix all the pheasant food four times a day – at 7am, 11am, 3pm and 7pm, from when the birds were day-olds till they went to wood at six weeks. The main foods were maize, biscuit meal and sieved boiled eggs. We had to stop on the rearing field till the birds were shut up and we were lucky if we were home by 10pm. You can imagine how tired we were as we trudged back home in the dark, with the owls hooting all about and every shadow regarded with suspicion.

'We also had to feed the hens and move the coops onto fresh ground every day. And each keeper had to run 50–60 traps.'

Harry remembers his time at Thornham with great affection. 'I knew it was a caring place from the day I arrived, when the headkeeper met me at the railway station with his pony and cart. As we drove the five miles to his house, travelling down narrow country roads, I saw thatched cottages with pink and cream-washed walls and I got the feeling that I had moved back in time by something like fifty years for I had not seen anything quite like it before.

'Over the next few days I met the rest of the keepers and, although we had dialect difficulties, and did so for quite some time, we all spoke "keepers' language". But I was in a completely different world: this was true country, untouched by anything modern – craftsmen carried out their duties using methods which had long vanished in the part of the North I had known. I saw men making large farm wagons and tumbrils, and farm methods and cropping were not the same. There were no heavy Shire horses and no hills, only flat ground. Even the weather was different, and, unless my memory is at fault, all the summers seemed to be warm and dry.

'The estate was in effect a country factory and everyone in the locality was

Rooks made a popular pie

employed by it, men of all professions, including foresters, sawyers, carpenters, painters and farmworkers. They even made their own bricks and field drains in moulds. The estate was self-supporting in every way and was owned and governed by a true country gentleman.

'Shooting took pride of place on the estate and dominated four days every other week. And during the Christmas period, when the boys were home from school, every day saw small parties enjoying the sport. Beaters were drawn from other departments on the estate so it really was a "family" outing.

'In those days the shooting men gave the keepers a party in one of the "locals" – there were two on the estate and it was held at each alternately. Those who had assisted the keepers – loaders, village policemen, head carpenter and so on – were also invited, and it was a time for everyone to let their hair down. Everyone contributed a song; the headkeeper always gave his favourite rendering of "The Galloping Major", and when it came to the "Bumpety-bumpety-bumpety-bump, as

Enthusiastic beating

though I was riding the charger" bit everyone went through the motions of doing so. We always had an extension of time so the party usually folded up at around 1am, which was considered just about the right length of time for everyone to have reached the stage when they were at least "happy" enough to walk home safely.

'Another party was held for the entire staff in the large, rambling servants' hall at the mansion, where all the married staff went for tea and all the single staff went for the evening's entertainment – a mixture of dancing and singing helped along with fairly liberal mugfuls of what was known locally as "owld beer", which either made you a little worse for wear or sobered you up, depending on what state you were in to begin with.

'Around midnight the family would come in and wish us all the compliments of the season. We would then all join hands to sing "Auld Lang Syne", and we meant every word of it.'

The present Lord Henniker was just a boy when Harry arrived from the North, but he vividly remembers that Grass was 'an excellent and enormously energetic keeper. Once, when walking with a senior keeper, he saw a bird he regarded as dangerous vermin – probably a magpie – and ran some two miles to his house to get a gun, then ran back and shot the bird. It was quite a feat. He was also immensely strong and regaled us with stories of his exploits at Cumbrian wrestling, at which he excelled in his youth.'

Harry turned his beat into the best on the estate and when John Palmer retired Harry took over as second keeper. Lord Henniker also said that when headkeeper John Chandler retired, Harry would take his place – but eleven years was too long for the ambitious Mr Grass to wait.

'One day a gentleman farmer came to see me and asked me to head a small two-keeper shoot between Bury St Edmunds and Newmarket. So off I went and made it the best shoot of its size in Suffolk, if not in England. And when the day came for me to resign, the owner, Mr Gittus, actually cried.

'The agent of Lord Milford of Dalham Hall, near Market, came to see me and invited me to go there as headkeeper. And I am pleased to say that I made it the finest pheasant shoot in all England. One day 1,200 pheasants came out from one drive – the North Field Belt – and the seven Guns killed only sixty-eight birds, such was their quality. Lord Milford said: "Grass, you've really excelled yourself today."'

Actually, the shoot already had an excellent reputation before Harry went there. Cecil Rhodes, founder of Rhodesia, purchased Dalham in 1900 because it was 'one of the best partridge shoots in England', and the first Lord Milford bought it from the Rhodes family in 1924 for the same reason, following the expiry of his lease at Six Mile Bottom.

Lord Milford's son, Major Philipps, recalled Harry's early days at Dalham in the 1940s. 'When I came home on embarkation leave I found the Derbyshire Yeomanry, with five of the best Shots in England, living in the house and shooting all the partridges. When I returned in 1945 there were no partridges, but Harry Grass had arrived and was rearing thousands of pheasants. All the farms were let at £1 per acre provided that they grew the crops required by Harry, never cut thistles before July and never used fertilizers or pesticides.'

Harry regarded Lord Milford as 'a great man', but 'he was so different from his son, Major Philipps. Matters came to a head one day when the Major was rude to my wife; I threatened to smack him in the mouth and decided to leave'.

Another job came along quickly, taking Harry to be the head of two keepers working for Lady Janet Bailey of Lake in Wiltshire. There his reputation continued to grow and after only one year Lord Mountbatten's agent, Commander North, came to see him and asked him to go to Broadlands in Hampshire as headkeeper.

Harry was 'signed on' by Lady Mountbatten, who at first declared that he could not spend much money as the shoot was at rock bottom. Not surprisingly, Harry, in his typically direct way, said 'I must have sufficient funds, but most of all I want my own way of doing things'. Fortunately, Lady Mountbatten agreed and said that Harry would be answerable to no one except her, not even the agent. The five other keepers would do whatever Harry required to build the shoot up.

As a result, on their first day, less than a year later, they killed more pheasants than in the whole of the previous season. Lady Mountbatten joined the party on the last drive before lunch and said to her husband: 'How are you getting on, dear?' He replied: 'We've already discovered one thing – Grass is not going to stand any nonsense.'

Thus the shoot's big build-up began, and it wasn't long before royal guests came from all over Europe to enjoy Broadlands' much talked about sport, at a time when big bags were still very much in vogue.

On Harry's best day ever, in 1968, they killed 2,139 pheasants on just four drives, and Prince Charles bagged 500! As usual, Harry blew his whistle to signal no more shooting after each drive, but after the last a single shot rang out. Harry told me 'I was so shocked, as my word was law and everyone knew it. So I marched over to the Guns to find out who the guilty party was. To my great surprise it was Prince Charles, and before I could say anything he said: "I'm sorry, but I'd killed 499 when the whistle went and I don't suppose I'll ever do that again." Still rather cross, I said to the prince: "Don't do it again, sir." "What?", he asked, "firing after the whistle?" "No, shoot 500 pheasants", I quipped, allowing a slight smile to creep across my face.'

News of the big bag travelled remarkably quickly and Harry recalls that within a few hours people were ringing up from as far away as Scotland, asking for all the details.

According to Harry, Prince Charles was then a much better Shot than the more experienced Prince Philip. When Prince Philip first went to Broadlands they shot 1,417 and he said to Harry: 'I bet you'll never do that again.' But Harry proudly recalls: 'The very next time he came we killed 1,600. There was no way I would allow standards to slip.'

Another famous guest was motoring mogul Henry Ford. One day he shot dangerously, at a partridge into the faces of the approaching beaters. Harry spun round to Lord Mountbatten and said 'Shall I go and warn him, sir?' The Earl replied: 'No, I'll get Lord Brabourne [Lord Mountbatten's son-in-law] to do it; he's a bit more diplomatic than you.'

Lord Mountbatten was 'a fair Shot', but to Harry he was 'a good employer, a good master and a real friend'. They travelled extensively together, Harry driving his master many hundreds of miles to other shoots.'We often stopped off at his London house on the way, and we always had the same for lunch – no discrimination.'

One famous shoot which they visited frequently was Sandringham, and it was on the royal estate that Harry mentioned to Lord Mountbatten that he had his retirement papers through. The Earl looked horrified and said to Harry: 'You're not going to retire: not only are you my keeper, but you are also my friend.' So Harry stayed on.

Lord Mountbatten's death at the hands of the IRA was a bitter blow to Harry, and with his friend and employer's passing the old keeper really lost his enthusiasm for almost everything. His sadness was as deep as his roots in keepering and he still remembers vividly how he joined the estate's other three heads of department in standing guard over Lord Mountbatten's coffin at the mansion. 'When you walked in you could have heard a pin drop, and when I looked up there were ladies with tears in their eyes.'

The estate passed to Lord Romsey, the Earl's grandson, who wanted to get rid of Broadlands' reputation as a 'blunderbuss' shoot, and instead concentrate on quality birds in smaller numbers. Of course, the young lord found it extremely difficult to follow in the footsteps of such a popular and loved employer. Harry found him 'altogether a different kettle of fish, and when, after a year or so, he suggested that I might retire, I did not find the decision difficult'.

Harry was given a small cottage at Broadlands for the rest of his life, along with a small pension. Today he grows a few tomatoes and cucumbers and sometimes goes to watch on shooting days, occasionally 'waving a white flag to get the birds up a bit'. And each Thursday he still drives his old Ford the seven miles to Romsey to help out in the gunshop there.

'Yes', said Harry emphatically, when I asked him if he would follow the keeper's path if he had his time over again. And he proudly proclaims that the family tradition continues. One day at Broadlands Prince Charles turned to Harry's grandson, Ian Brown, and said: 'Are you going to be a keeper like your grandfather?' Then he turned to Harry and said: 'Grass – he'll start at Broadlands', which in due course he did.

Much of Harry's sound advice was once regularly recorded in the pages of *Shooting Times*, the editor having asked him to contribute a monthly page in the late seventies and early eighties. He always wrote in longhand and persuaded one of the ladies in the Broadlands estate office to type each piece, but his style was excellent and needed very little editing.

Harry's subject matter ranged far and wide, from rearing to roosting, from predation to tipping. The biggest tip he ever received was '£40 from a foreigner, but the average in my last few years at Broadlands was £10. And royals always

1880's

The "Viscount" Ventilating Shooting Boot

Under the patronage of

The Right Hon. the Earl of Cork and Orrery (the Master of Her Majesty's Buck Hounds).
The Right Hon. Lord Henry Thynne.
The Right Hon. Viscount Dungarvan.
The Right Hon. Viscount Weymouth.

PATENTED.

OPEN.—**A** Ventilating Air Tubes.

tipped much in line with the other guests. As is customary, I shared the tips out with the other keepers at the end of the season, unless there was a particularly good day, when it was done immediately. In the old days at Lambton we always thought that the headkeeper kept more than his fair share when it came to pay-out time. I suppose all keepers suspect their bosses.'

But Harry is particularly renowned for his success in dealing with poachers. And he had to be specially vigilant at Broadlands, which is so easily accessible by a number of major roads and only a few miles from Southampton and other towns.

Unfortunately, a lifetime's zeal has taken its toll, and today Harry gets about only with the aid of a stick. He fell and broke his knee eighteen years ago while rushing to get his pheasants in during a thunderstorm, and this obviously still troubles him today.

While working for Sir Arthur Wood at The Hermitage a poacher stabbed him in the thigh and lower leg and he needed ten stitches. A friend advised him to learn how to wrestle and box, and this he did with a vengeance, eventually becoming one of the most feared keepers of his generation. He took lessons once or twice a week from the amateur champion of Cumberland and Westmorland style wrestling. When he could pin down and throw his tutor he went to another amateur champion to learn how to box, becoming very proficient at that, too. He was a match for anyone.

Harry was only eleven when he gave evidence against a poacher for the first time. He was on his way home from school when he saw one of the Lambton keepers chasing a man with a .410. Later the headkeeper was consulted and it was decided that, despite his tender years, Harry was sufficiently mature to identify the poacher in court. And afterwards, the magistrate congratulated him on the clear way he gave evidence.

As the years went by Harry became increasingly tough with the many poachers he apprehended and had no hesitation in 'giving them a good hiding'. Once a gypsy threatened Harry with a knife, but the fearless keeper had no trouble in seizing the weapon. 'I cut off the tip of his nose with it and said: "There, every time you look in the mirror you'll remember me and think twice about coming here again!"'

At Henniker's the keepers went nightwatching in groups of three, their shifts being from dusk till 1am, and 1am till dawn. Anyone caught was taken to the local police station. Harry and his colleagues never called in the police to help apprehend poachers, as is the modern, more cautious, practice.

On another occasion, at Broadlands, Harry came across a group of eight poachers, a couple of whom gave him 'a lot of lip' as they all made off. Shortly afterwards, a local farmer called Harry in to deal with two poachers, one of whom turned out to be 'the lippy one', and Harry had no hesitation in giving him a good thrashing.

At Henry Bell's, Harry once found a revolver left behind by a poacher, whom he recognised as the local Italian ice-cream seller. 'When I went in and slapped the gun down on his counter you should have seen the look on his face.'

Harry himself never carried a revolver, but he always had a home-made truncheon, two of which he still has among many shoot relics.

Despite all his fighting expertise, Harry did not go to the front in the last war. Instead, he was a sergeant in the Home Guard at Bury St Edmunds. The closest he

The popular press nicknamed Harry Grass 'King of the Gamekeepers'. Here he is pictured outside his Broadlands cottage in 1988, with one of the old truncheons he used to keep for protection

ever came to hostilities was when two planes crashed on his shoot, 'one of ours and one of theirs, and both pilots were killed'.

However, he saw death twice in the shooting field. One accident took place at Lord Iveagh's famous Elveden shoot near Thetford, in headkeeper Turner's time, when Harry was loading for Major Philipps. The loader for a neighbouring Gun accidentally shot the second keeper in the stomach and he was dead before they reached him. Later they learned that this was the first time the careless man had acted as a loader.

While such horrific incidents often persuaded lesser men to take up safer, less adventurous occupations, Harry never wavered in his love of the keepering life. Not only was he the friend and confidant of kings and commoners, he was himself a king, the absolute ruler of fine sporting estates and the terror of those who would steal his game.

Note: Sadly, Harry Grass died in May 1990.

LEN MACEY

Dorset and Hampshire

When five Ilsington keepers marched out of Dorset to fight Hitler's war few members of that very rural community would have guessed that only one would return. This lucky man was headkeeper Leonard Macey, who immediately went back to the life which meant so much to him. After the long 'apprenticeship' customary in those days, he had proudly followed in his father's footsteps in ruling the roost on Mr Wilfred Brymer's estate near Puddletown. And not surprisingly, both sides of his family had keepering in their blood.

Born in June 1909, Len left school at the age of fourteen, in August. 'My mate was coming up next day to play Indians with me. But when I went home to tea father said "Mr Thomson, the agent, wants you bird scaring at 7s 6d a week. And remember, rooks eat corn on Sundays as well as Mondays". There was little I could do: in those days you couldn't argue and no one expected anything different.

'When I started work I also did a bit of corn thrashing and gradually started to help father with the pheasant feeding. I was good at breaking eggs, too', said Len with a twinkle in his eye. 'You see, most of the time all we had to put pheasant eggs in was our baggy trouser pockets, and when we bent down they often tumbled out.

'The trouble with today is that the keepers don't get no apprenticeship like we had: nowadays they are all headkeepers before they even start. But I had to follow the established system typical of any large estate then. First you became kennel boy for twelve months, and then, if you behaved yourself, you were sent out with an underkeeper and he could box your ears, tan your hide and do anything he liked.

'After two or three years I was given my own small beat, which I used to patrol with a 16-bore. I was given three dozen gin traps and told "There's your vermin". And with all the surrounding estates so well keepered we really had the vermin under control.

'Of course, there were no ready-made feed pellets in those days and, like everyone else, we used to cook and mix our own. We always started with scalded biscuit meal – not too much water – just enough to bring it up nicely. Then we would cook rice – just a little so that it was still firm, and then sieve and grade it. Seeds were later added as required. We also used the juice from scalded rabbit meat, which was put through a mincer. Actually, I was much better with a pair of choppers and really had it off to a fine art.

'We often spent between a half and three-quarters of an hour in food preparation four times a day. As the birds got older they were put on hemp and other seeds. And you had to feed according to the weather, adding more moisture in dry conditions.

Len Macey remembers when large numbers of wildfowl came to southern rivers every winter

'The coops were twenty-five yards apart and there were twenty yards between the rows. And what some work it was putting out three hundred coops with eighteen birds to a coop. All the coops were exactly the same size and made by the estate's three full-time carpenters.

'In those days the pheasant was a really wild bird and flew well naturally at only a few weeks old. Now they don't know how to fly at eight months! Only last season when I was at . . . I said to the boss: "Look, they're having to fly so high for the first time in their lives they're trembling, poor things".

'Hot weather brought real trouble, for when the birds came out of the coops to get cool they were straight off for the rest of the day if you went anywhere near them. I can't imagine how many hours we spent nursing those birds. Many's the time we finished penning the birds in our best clothes at nine or ten o'clock at night so that we could go straight to the local dance. And many's the night I didn't get away at all, but was up listening to the church clock strike one . . . two . . .

'Birds were always put to wood at six weeks, not eight as became the fashion. They were a real handful on the open field. If a thunderstorm came up you were really in trouble.

'Mr Brymer was a true country squire who really lived for the estate and hated London. He was a very particular man and we always used to say you could feel his eyes through a door. I liked him though. There were certain unwritten laws on the estate, and as long as you abided by them you did all right:

'When I first started, the beaters were given two or three shillings a day, or a shilling for boys under fifteen, but by the mid-Twenties this had risen to five shillings. And everyone, beaters and keepers, was given a packed lunch prepared by my mother, who had an allowance of 1s 7d per person. It was always bread and cheese, a beef sandwich and a bottle of beer – light or dark ale – which cost 7d. Boys were given lemonade, or hot cocoa if lunch was near the house. And sometimes it was all laid out on a table.

'Nobody seemed to be in such a damned hurry then. Don't forget you had to walk everywhere, and if you had a horse and cart to hop aboard you were lucky. The Guns went to the big house for a slap-up lunch of course, but sometimes ate in a special marquee. It was quite a palaver, with a proper luncheon car – a great shooting-brake. First the butler came down with all the hardware, and later the ladies came out just in time for lunch. And they generally stayed to watch the afternoon sport.

'For the Guns there was no fixed time for lunch, but keepers and beaters always had to be away smartly to sort out the blanking in: much as it is today really, though any good shoot captain always ensures the Guns are on parade at the right time.

'I can only just remember beaters wearing smocks on one or two very old-fashioned shoots, but not on our estate. Many were unemployed lads from Dorchester, who always came in heavy greatcoats. Of course we knew they popped the odd bird in their pockets or hid them to collect later. And some even set wires throughout the three-day shoots.

'With the beaters, one thing in particular we had to watch was when they were paid. I had to make sure that as each man came up he went to a separate line as, given half a chance, he would come round for a double whack, insisting that he hadn't had his yet.

'In those days estates like ours were like little empires and most of the staff never expected to live or work anywhere else. Many of us, including footmen and chauffeur as well as keepers, had a family house and that would be ours till death or departure.

'The six-mile-long estate covered 8,000 acres when Brymer died in 1957, but now it is down to some 2,000', reflected Len sadly. 'When you had such a big estate it was quite obvious which were the best parts for shoot-

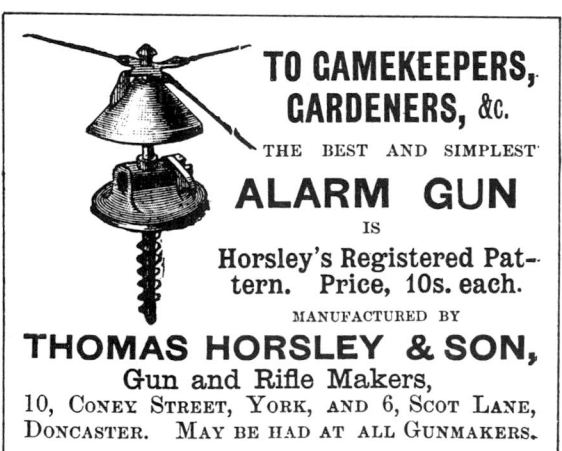

One day in 1927, when Len Macey keepered on Wilfred Brymer's estate, near Puddletown, Dorset

ing, and when all these empires were broken up I felt sorry for the poor devils who took on the bad bits.

'Ours was mostly partridge ground, but we had pheasants too, and up to the last war there were six of us to deal with them. But when hostilities broke out everyone was encouraged to join the TA, and when the TA keepers went down to their meetings there were only two of us left to feed. And with the estate workers gone I had to help out with farming and forestry. In the end five of us keepers joined up – I went in the RAF for six years – and four never came back.

'When war broke out we had 6,000 birds on the estate so shooting must have been quite good for a while, though the vermin problem would have increased rapidly. But with the shortages, cartridges soon became a problem. Spent cases were kept and we managed to get some re-loads done at Winchester, but only in small quantities.

'In those days keepers always wanted to better themselves of course, and in this I suppose I was particularly lucky. My father suddenly became ill and was dead within three days. Mr Brymer said: "You can take his job provided you get married!" So I did.

'After the war he really wanted me back to pick up where we had left off, and he put me on the payroll in October 1945, even though I was still being paid by the Government. And for two years I was more or less on my own, killing vermin. But we were just getting organised with underkeepers and rearing again when Mr Brymer died, in 1957.

'A farmers' syndicate took on the shooting, but I didn't like it so decided to move. In those days there were always several pages of vacancies plus several pages of situations-wanted ads in *The Gamekeeper*, but by then I was fifty-two and decided to play safe by placing the same job-wanted ad in local newspapers in half-a-dozen southern counties. As a result I wrote to four estates and got on three shortlists. In those days nobody would take you without a reference, and many even wanted one for your wife – if she was a dirty slut you'd had it.

'Eventually I went to Arnold Laver's Longwood estate, near Winchester in Hampshire, where Sir Brian Mountain of Eagle Star had the shooting over about 4,000 acres, and I remained there till cutbacks forced me to retire in 1974. At first I had three underkeepers.

'When Laver died Sir Brian wanted to buy the estate, but I believe he was outbid by Ronnie Lyon, who just kept his hand up at the auction, to the tune of 3½ million. But Lyon was stretched with a lot of other property and business interests and after just eighteen months went into voluntary liquidation.

'Sir Brian was a nice fellow. He never interfered with us, but always expected good shooting. The funny thing is that on our first day together we didn't get off to a good start. He said to me: "Macey, I expect to wait ten minutes for my first birds after lunch", but unfortunately the underkeeper misunderstood my orders, took in more ground than required and poor old Sir Brian had to wait thirty minutes. Of course I apologised, but after that everything was all right.

'In my youth a one hundred-bird day was good and a four hundred-bird day marvellous for the keepers as all the Guns then came forward with a ha'penny tip. Of course, the tips going to the headkeeper were always a bone of contention, but we always split them equally. Hare shoots were very profitable for us as there were so many Guns out.

'But the Mountains expected only a few hundred birds a day. Once I did get up to nine hundred, but thought that far too many. I really think big bags are quite unnecessary today.

'Sir Brian also had a much bigger shoot at Dunley in Hampshire, where all the important guests went. I always used to say that when a customer came through the door the amount of money he was going to spend determined which of the two shoots he would be invited to.

'When I started for Mr Brymer before the war it had been an entirely different scene and everything had revolved around the social circle. Then, guests almost always stayed in the house and we always looked after them well, including cleaning their guns.'

Today Len Macey remains in very good health and has excellent recollection of special days, some right back in his childhood. In particular he has many happy memories of the River Frome, which ran through the Ilsington Estate for two miles. No mallard or hen pheasants were ever shot after Christmas, but wigeon and teal were shot by the hundred, especially in cold weather. 'And when the Russians got stuck into the Finns in 1939 it must have frightened all the duck up there as we had the best season ever. That was the year I fell in the river.

'Once in late April we had a tremendous snowstorm and all the pheasants were buried by a great drift up against the corrugated iron side of the pen. Luckily we

Len Macey outside his cottage at Owslebury, Hampshire in 1988

could see the little air holes they had melted, and managed to dig most of them out unharmed.

'Snow was also a menace at holiday time. We were only ever given one week's holiday – if we were lucky – and that would be in February. But that wasn't always much good because if a blizzard struck we couldn't go anywhere.

'One year we had a real arctic week and the river was all frozen up. In one little three- or four-acre meadow the water had broken the bank and the ground was packed with snipe as thick as starlings. So I rushed up to the guv'nor and he managed to assemble three or four Guns. The birds just wouldn't go away, especially them little jack snipe, and we could have shot hundreds. But we thought enough was enough and stopped at eighty. Anyway we always had a lot of snipe driving. Now those days are long gone, with the drainage so well controlled and most of the marsh habitat sacrificed to corn.

'Generally in those days everyone was happy if we shot enough for the house and for the guests and friends to take a brace or two home – pot-hunting really. Now, of course, nobody can afford to get their dinner in this way.

'Poaching was not too bad in Dorset, but later, at Longwood, we had quite a few problems with people shooting from cars along the road. Most Dorset folk were in work so there was no real necessity or great aggravation. Father always used to say

Len Macey's mementoes include this trap for catching-up pheasants. Made in Dorset in the 1920s, it was sprung when a pheasant, attracted by feed sprinkled beneath, hopped onto the bent hazel branch

Another of Len Macey's keepering mementoes is this pair of bellows (circa 1930) used for puffing powder into the coops when pheasants were suffering from gapes

to anyone he caught: "Look Jack, if it's one for the family that's all right, but don't come too often".

'We had special names for most of the regular poachers – I can still see their faces now, especially old Joby White. One day I met him hobbling up the road on sticks, and he told me how a pipe had fallen on him when he was helping with PLUTO, the pipeline under the ocean which was laid to supply oil to the fleet. Sadly, the accident had permanently damaged his spine, but with that same old twinkle in his eyes he looked up and said: "At least you won't have to chase me any more".

'Poaching became much more of a problem after the war because there just weren't enough keepers to guard everything. In the old days I can remember counting over a hundred bona fide full-time keepers at the local hunt dinner, but when we came back from the war I looked around the tables and there was just me and one other. Once we had neighbours over every hill, but in 1946 the nearest keeper was twelve miles away.

'We had some real characters among the Guns too. One peppery old colonel was shooting so badly he blamed the turnips in which he was standing, so he kicked them out of the ground to form a six-foot circle. Unfortunately, he still missed virtually everything. And on another occasion his dog was attached to his waist by a very long string. At the end of one very hectic drive with birds whizzing all over the place he was bound up just like a mummy.

'But there were some really good Shots too. I well remember one day when I stood with Colonel Weaver along the Frome. He shot a good teal cleanly and turned to shoot another, but before the first hit the water a peregrine dashed in and took it. The Colonel declared: "If I'd another barrel I'd have stopped him, too!"'

Like so many of his kind, Len Macey was in great demand to help out on neighbouring estates when he stopped full-time keeping. And he leapt at the chance to stay busy: 'Any man who's been active all his life just can't suddenly cut off – he might as well sign up with the undertaker'. Even today Len manages to drive himself around to pick-up three or four days a week on five estates.

Len's son did not follow him into keepering – 'The good days were over'. But talking to Len today it is quite obvious how much he enjoyed his career and I am sure he would do it all over again. 'They were hard times, but as long as you looked forward two months all the time you never got into too much of a muck, and then you had twelve months full of interest.'

When we looked back through Len's old photograph album he could still recall every detail as if it were yesterday: all the dimensions of the pens, the names of long-dead friends and much, much more. One particularly interesting little snap showed a full-grown rabbit and six dead day-old pheasant chicks which had *all* been taken from the mouth of a fox which Len shot while it was on the way back to its den and cubs. This was just one of those many relatively unimportant, but nonetheless fascinating incidents which Len, and others like him, will always remember.

'I've had a grand time keepering', he told me. 'Up at six to see miles of fog all down the valley – just the odd tree or steeple poking through – that's what I call life.'

Long may Len and his wife continue to enjoy their 'retirement', their country life and treasured memories at Longwood, near Owslebury, in Hampshire's rural heartland.

1931

WALLY FAKES
Norfolk and Hampshire

'I think my family has been in keepering ever since game preservation first started', Wally Fakes told me at his country cottage in pretty little Preston Candover, near New Alresford, Hampshire. Christened Walter Henry on 20 May 1902, Wally has indeed carried out a considerable amount of research into his family tree and one of his proudest possessions is a painting of his grandfather, who was headkeeper at Livermere, Suffolk.

When Wally was born at Hilborough, between Swaffham and Brandon 'in the cream of Norfolk shooting country', his father was second keeper (later headkeeper) for Joseph Truman-Mills, and there was little doubt over the career Wally would follow. He was destined to serve three generations of Truman-Mills and two of Cheshams.

Not everyone was so lucky, though. 'Unless you was a keeper's or shepherd's son you wouldn't have had a job in those parts. Each village was more or less entire in itself – a little kingdom, and if you took a job there, by golly you kep' it.'

Wally started as a boy assistant aged fourteen, on the day he left school, at 'the fine pay of fourteen bob a week'. In those days a headkeeper received about £1 a week and a farm workers 12s 6d. 'But the head did have quite a few perks, such as guns and two ton of coal a year, and there was none of them income tax rules what there is now.'

His first duties were mostly concerned with helping the warreners with rabbiting in winter and assisting the keepers in the rearing season. Not until he was twenty did a vacancy arise, enabling him to have his own beat under his father, as one of a team of four plus one 'yard boy'.

'All the estate's coops were confined to one or two fields, and between the wars there were about six hundred of them, all made by the estate carpenter, and each beat keeper was assigned his share to look after. There were twenty-five yards between the rows and twenty-one yards between each coop, and each coop had a young spruce bough cut in half and placed inside so that the chicks could hide in the foliage. The estate carpenter also made all the nestboxes, and the coops were limewashed (with Coopic mixed in) every year, by the bricklayer at the end of each season.'

Each keeper was given one suit of clothes one year and a pair of boots the next, but in later years, when he worked for the Cheshams, Wally was to receive a suit every year, but no boots.

'We placed nineteen eggs under each hen, seventeen if it was a small one. An

Wally Fakes has no son to continue his family's great keepering tradition

average of about sixteen birds per coop went to wood and we reckoned on shooting ten birds per coop, plus wild birds of course.'

He followed the typical feeding system of the day, starting the birds off with a base mix of sieved hardboiled eggs and barley meal. Biscuit meal was added at about two weeks, and after that rice, wheat, hempseed and so on, as the birds grew bigger. Feeds were given every day at 6am, 10am, 2pm and 6pm. And with a little run in front of each coop the birds soon became tame.

'Mind you, they *was* pheasants then', said Wally proudly, 'and they could fly as soon as they had wings.' Naturally, they needed considerable care and were shut up each night till they were three weeks old; after this the coops were left open.

There were always two men on nightwatching duty, a keeper and a summer help, so it worked out that each man was up every third night. 'The headkeeper never did anything like that.'

Each day on the rearing field was followed by a day on the partridge beat, so there was little time for rest. 'In fact the only time you was off the beat was when you was on the rearing field.

'Snow was quite a problem in those days and the estate kept a plough to keep the roads open – this was also used to run a track along the fences as this was where we would trickle a little feed for the partridges.

'Each beat had six dozen traps, the old four-inch gin – things was done properly then. But apart from the vermin, everything was in favour of game then. There was no such thing as sprays. The corn was simply set and rolled and the gate shut till harvest. The only variable was the weather.

'Henry Truman-Mills inherited from his father, Joseph, and was known as HT. He didn't live at the shoot, but had an estate at Market Harborough and always came down with his guests on the train to Brandon Station, about nine miles away. A covered wagon was always sent to collect them, and their very considerable luggage. They were always four-day shoots to begin with, going down to three days later in the season.

'Bags were much bigger then, of course, and HT's birthday was always an occasion for a one thousand-bird day. Pheasants and partridges were driven together starting at the end of October, and generally there were only three drives in the morning and one in the afternoon.

'In a good partridge year there were two sets of beaters. They wore stone-coloured smocks with red collars and most were local farmworkers. For lunch each man was given about a quarter pound of cheese, a roll and a pint of beer, and was paid about half-a-crown a day, payable on the last day of the shoot.

'The keepers' lunch was always cooked: on three days we went to tenant farmers' houses, and on the fourth to the headkeeper's. Do you know, I never had a beer till I was twenty-five, and then that was only because they left the ginger beer behind. The Guns' grub was sent from a local pub to one of the houses of the tenant farmers.

'It really was a very isolated part of the world then. Apart from the guest Guns and one or two visiting relatives, we never saw a stranger from one year to the next. Cars were still very rare and when I went to school before World War I you could play hopscotch and marbles and run a hoop down the road in total safety. Not now though: I've been back and there's a car in every gateway.

'There was no real trouble with poachers until cars came along – in fact incidents were so unusual I can still remember the first occasion we had to get the police out, to a gang of four from Norwich. But I was never attacked. In any case, they couldn't have hit me with a handful of rice: I was too fast. However, I always carried a swingle in my pocket – just in case.'

Wally says he only ever had two real frights. 'The first was in the days before I got married, and I don't mind telling you my hair absolutely stood on end. I went to feed the woods at dusk during the shooting season. It was just about dark and I was on my way back to my bike across the Marsnage, a rough, old place with patches of bog and gorse, where there was a lot of grazing and some horses turned out.

'I could see like a cat in those days and not a lot could surprise me. But suddenly, as I turned, something white flashed right before my face and at the same time gave a great sigh. I could feel my hat lift. But when I saw that it was only a horse with a white blaze, by God I swore. I readily admit I was truly startled. Simple as that.

'The other scare which stands out in my memory was when I ran through the River Wissey to get away from an ol' bull – it was the only place to go and fortunately I could get right across, because he was waitin' for me. Mind you, he

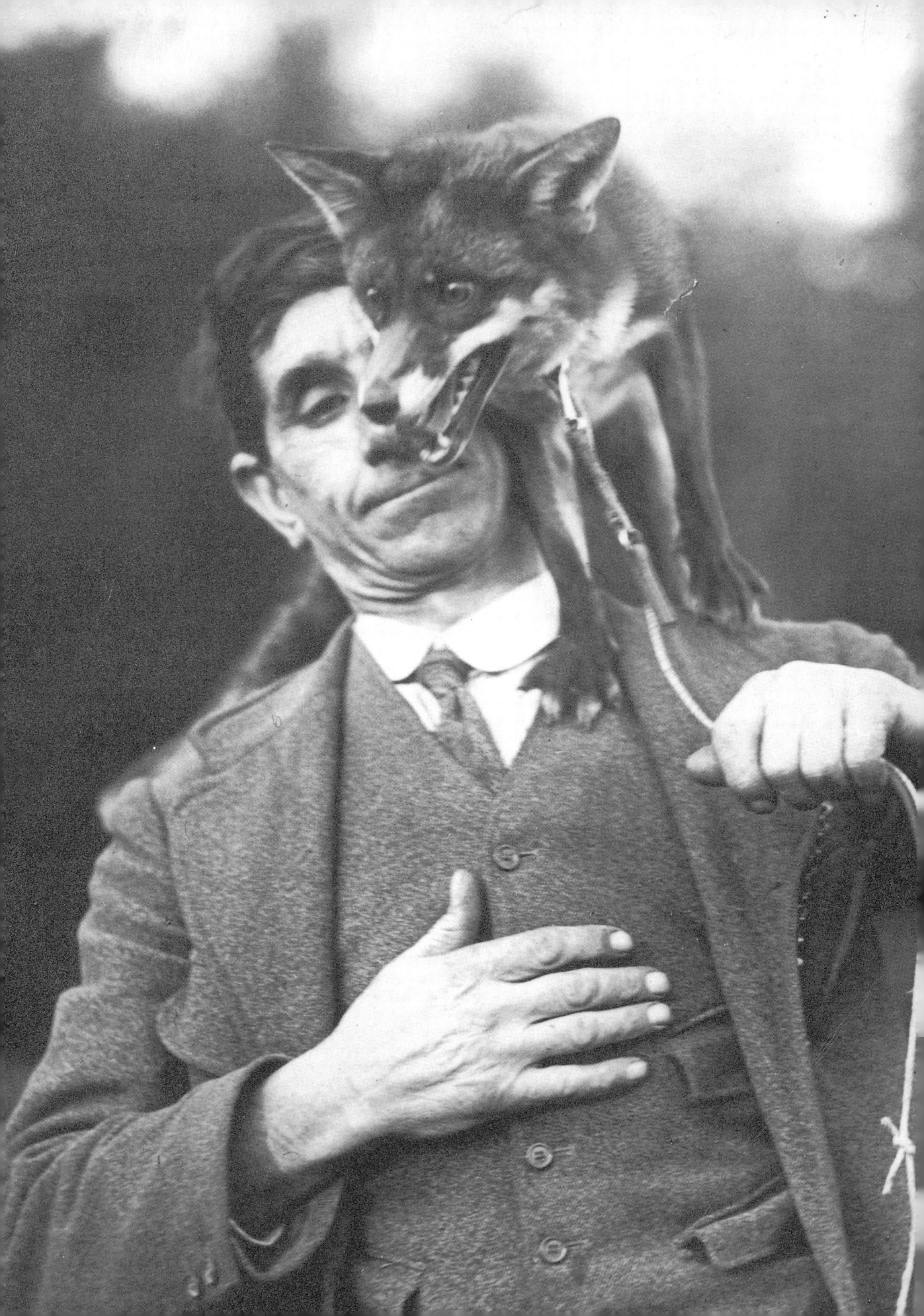

was as lucky as me because I had a gun under my arm and by golly I would have used it if I'd been snarled up!'

Later, as he had no children, HT left the estate to his nephew CT; after a year Wally decided to take advantage of CT's generous offer of a £104 pay-off for anyone who left and had been with the estate for two years. The Truman-Mills had married into the Cavendish family, and it was arranged for Wally to go to Lord Chesham's at Latimer, Chesham, Buckinghamshire in 1934, the nest-egg enabling him to get married in the same year. As second keeper he earned good money, 38s a week which soon increased to £2, considerably more than a farm worker had 'at a time when money had real spending power, when coal was half-a-crown a hundredweight and sugar twopence a pound'.

Wally was to stay at Latimer till 1956, apart from four years during the war, when he 'tramped the bloody Sahara from Algiers to Tunis as a stretcher bearer'. He had wanted to use a gun – 'I could knock a gnat's eye out with a rifle' – but at forty-two was told that he was too old. Lord Chesham appealed on his behalf, but to no avail.

Soon after the war headkeeper Jack West retired and Wally took over, heading a team of four. But in 1956 the Cheshams sold Latimer, after it had been in the family for some 400 years, and Wally went to Brockwood, the Chesham's Hampshire estate.

Thus life went peacefully on for Mr and Mrs Fakes and in 1979 Wally's loyal service was recognised at the CLA Game Fair at Bowood, when Prince Charles presented him with the sixty-year long-service award. 'It was the hottest day of my life, but of course you had to have your jacket and tie on. Prince Charles said to me: "Have you really done sixty years?" and I said "Yes, your Highness, but actually I've done sixty-three!"'

Wally stopped full-time keepering when he had done sixty-five years, but carried on part-time till he was eighty-four. During this time he carried on loading for Lord Chesham, accompanying him to many other shoots. For example, they used to go to aviator Tommy Sopwith's moor at Arkengarthdale for a week each year. 'Once one of the Guns didn't turn up and I was invited to shoot. Lord Chesham kindly gave me one of his guns. It was a shade too long for me, but I took my jacket off and I done well.'

Not surprisingly, Wally always did a fair bit of shooting and counted pigeon shooting as one of his hobbies, carrying on till 1987. 'Several days I've topped the hundred', he told me.

He also still remembers a day during the war when he went boar shooting in Tunisia. 'I was the brigadier's bodyguard and he was invited out for the day by the local French officers, who ran the place. We were standing among some cork oaks when he said "You might as well have a go". I didn't get anything, but afterwards we had a wonderful meal with the French and there was much singing of *viva la compagnie* late into the night. Oh yes, they weren't all bad days, like.'

Jack West was Lord Chesham's headkeeper before Wally Fakes took over, just after the war. His pet fox had been found on the estate as a cub and he raised it on a bottle

Although they have been in their present cottage for seventeen years, the Fakes have had seven cottages with the Cheshams. Wally has no regrets in staying with the same family for so long – 'After all, you always keep with them what you know. And I am proud to say that Lord Chesham counts me as a friend.

'There are just two things I would have liked as a beginner: the Fenn trap instead of the gin and food pellets instead of all that mixing. Everything's against game production now, but at least I can say I knew it at its best. We never minded the long hours and the low pay – we gloried in it – yes!'

In his retirement Wally is well looked after by Lord Chesham, and Mrs Stella Fakes still works three mornings a week doing domestic work for Lady Chesham and helping her with dinner parties. But their only son (a bachelor) has broken the family connection with keepering. He is a consultant engineer with British Rail and travels all over the world – a far cry from father's very parochial days in Norfolk.

The Fakes keepering dynasty may have ended, but Wally still has that unmistakable twinkle of the game preserver in his watchful eye.

Note: Sadly, Wally Fakes passed away peacefully on 21 October, 1989.

Wally Fakes outside his country cottage in 1988

BILL GILL
Wintershall, Surrey

William Henry Gill is one of those rare individuals who have devoted their entire working lives to single estates. For over fifty-one years he has served only two masters, and apart from the war, when he was stationed abroad to fight for king and country, he has always lived at Selhurst Common, within the surprisingly unspoilt labyrinth of narrow lanes which cut through the gentle hills to the east of Godalming, in Surrey.

Bill was born on 5 January 1919, the son of a keeper who had worked on several local estates, and the grandson of a well-digger. But his father was working in forestry when Bill left Grafham School at the age of fourteen, so it was to a neighbouring estate, Sir Keith Price's Wintershall, that Bill went to work as underkeeper. Before that, his only experience of keepering had been working with his chums as stops, for 2s 6d each on Saturdays.

He became one of a team of three and his starting wage was 22s 6d for a seven-day week. Harry Smithers was the head and his son Herbert was second keeper.

In those early Thirties the land was more hospitable to both game and wildlife: the fields were much smaller and there were many more hedgerows. The roads were tarmacked, but each section was in the permanent care of one man who took great pride in his work and got to know local people well. Indeed, it was in the roadman's interests to befriend the keepers as he was given a shilling for each gamebird nest reported along the roadside. The eggs were then taken and placed under broody hens along with the others in the care of the keeper.

As junior keeper, Bill spent much of his time ministering to the needs of the broodies, in particular cleaning them out. Some fifty hens were bought from local farmers in April, as soon as the pheasants started laying, and they cost about half a crown each. Nestboxes were placed in units of six, each hen covering some 19–21 eggs according to her size, and all were positioned on specially created banks so that the keepers did not have to bend too much in tending them. Shade, too, was a very important consideration as too much heat disturbed the sitting birds.

When the chicks hatched after about three weeks, they were placed in a basket, and the hen in a sack over the keeper's shoulder, and the whole family taken to a coop in the rearing field. The coops were in rows thirty yards (27m) apart, and they were moved every other day to keep the ground reasonably fresh. Inside each run the keepers placed some boughs for the chicks to hide in when danger threatened, for example when a hawk loomed overhead.

Regular feeding times were 6 and 10am and 2 and 6pm, the birds being shut into the coops after the last feed. Bill recalls how quiet he had to be when approaching

Bill Gill, pictured here with his boss Peter Hutley (right), on his last shoot day before retiring at the end of the 1983/84 season

each coop as, at the slightest noise, the birds would bolt out and take much precious time to round up. And the older the chicks were, the more troublesome they became.

The usual diet of scalded biscuit meal, boiled rice, barley and oatmeal, maize etc was mixed and boiled up in an eight-gallon pot boiler in the rearing-field hut, where all the bags of feed were kept. It took about three-quarters of an hour to prepare each feed and Bill always knew when the mix was right as 'it fell apart easily when dropped'.

The field hut measured 12 by 8ft (3.6 by 2.4m), and along one side ran a bench, on which the keeper could sleep. 'In fact from May to August, I only went home at weekends for a change of clothes', said Bill. 'We worked all the hours God made, but we was lucky as poaching was never much of a problem in this area, just the odd pot-shot from a car along the lanes. Mind you though, Harry Smithers was hit on the head with an iron bar when he stepped out of his back door one night. But even then, no one ever knew whether it was a poacher who attacked him.'

Every evening, as well as locking the birds up, Bill had to go out and shoot half-a-dozen rabbits, which he then had to gut, skin and mince up ready to add to the early-morning feed.

In addition, each keeper had to check thirty to forty ginns twice a day. The small traps took stoats and weasels, and the six-inch ginns caught foxes. For the latter, Bill would lay a cluster of four ginns – 'north, south, east and west' – and bait the centre with the strong-smelling body of a cat, also taken in a gin. Badgers, too, were commonly taken in ginns, but birds of prey, including owls, were taken in pole traps, long since rightly outlawed.

It was relatively easy to ensure that birds were released to wood in batches as the eggs could be kept fresh for up to about three weeks by standing them in corn and turning them every day.

When release time came – by mid-August – the poults were taken to the wood by horse and wagon, unless the coops happened to be near the release point, when they would be moved towards it in stages.

There was relatively little disease because the keepers were scrupulously attentive to hygiene: this meant endless scrubbing and washing of equipment and regular movement of coops onto fresh ground. There was the usual occasional outbreak of gapes, but Bill used his father's remedy for this: spirits of camphor and gentian were obtained from the local chemist and added to the birds' feed at the rate of one tablespoon per one hundred pheasants. Of course, this had to be thoroughly mixed in, but usually did the trick and the birds coughed up the dead gape worms. In a very bad case, a drop of the medicine was applied to a ball of food and forced down the sick bird's throat. As Bill said, 'this either killed or cured them', but the casualties were 'only about one in ten'.

At the time Bill wore cord breeches, pigskin leggings, ankle-length boots and a thornproof tweed jacket 'which really was impervious to rain – you could stop out in it all day!' His first suit, traditionally provided by his employer, cost just £7 10s, but by 1960 this had risen to £15 10s, and his last – in 1983 – cost £230. In earlier days this was topped by a tweed cap, but in later years he changed to a trilby.

His employer was Keith Price, who had a match factory in Sweden; he was 'a reasonable Shot' but insisted on using all-brass cartridges, 'and they was mighty heavy to carry about I can tell you', Bill remembered ruefully.

Sir Keith also rented the adjoining Nore shoot, where there were quite a few English partridges at the time. They started shooting these in October, but bags were never more than ten to twenty brace, along with a few pheasants. Main pheasant days were in the hundred-bird range – fairly small compared with today, 'but the boss was more interested in enjoyment than numbers'.

Lunch was always an important consideration and taken at a regular time. The keepers and beaters went to a special lunch hut, where they dined well on a big joint of beef or leg of bacon plus bread and cheese, all provided by the estate. 'There was also a big tub of beer, a wooden barrel, and everyone helped themselves.' Meanwhile, the Guns – a traditional mix of local guests and business contacts – went to the big house for more refined fare.

There were about fifteen beaters in the Thirties and they started on 6s a day, later rising to 7s. They were always easy to get: nine or ten came from the Wintershall

The beating team on Bill Gill's last day

estate, including three woodmen as well as farm workers.

Guest Guns were sent on their way with the usual brace of birds apiece, and the bulk of the bag was then sold to the local butcher, 6s a brace being the lowest price in those days.

Bill was called up in 1939 and first posted to India. As a sergeant in the Queen's, the worst fighting he encountered was against the Afghans on the North-West Frontier, but the going was also very tough against the Japanese in the Burmese jungle, where Bill found his country upbringing a great advantage.

Meanwhile, Harry Smithers and his son stayed on the estate, Harry because he was too old to fight and Herbert in the reserved occupation of farm worker. Thus the shoot continued in a reasonable state and some sport was enjoyed during the war years, unlike on many estates where lack of manpower meant no vermin control or rearing at all.

It was snowing when Bill arrived back at Stoughton Barracks, Guildford, at Christmas 1945. There he stayed for just one night before making the short journey, in his demob suit, over to Wintershall where he rejoined the same team of keepers in the same pecking order.

In the following year Bill married Gladys, a local girl, and in due course they had two sons, though neither has entered the keepering profession.

Sir Keith Price still owned Wintershall, but his health was failing. 'He was a real gentleman', said Bill, 'and always walked around the estate to visit every employee's cottage every Sunday morning.'

When Price died there was a gap of a year or so before Peter Hutley became the new owner. Bill had served Sir Keith for three decades, but this new partnership proved to be equally successful and stood the test of a further two decades.

When Harry Smithers died his son took over as headkeeper, and when Herbert left to work for Sir Keith Price's son at Chiddingfold, Bill was left to run the shoot on his own. But there was less land to manage as the Nore shoot had been lost, and parts of Wintershall sold off to raise money for death duties.

Later on Peter Hutley started to add to the estate, and for the four years prior to his retirement at the end of the 1983/84 season, Bill was assisted by Simon Jelley, who eventually took over and is still at Wintershall today. Now they rear over 5,000 pheasants and 1,600 duck. Not surprisingly, Bill regrets the trend towards achieving consistently large bags – more recently the estate lets quite a few days to discerning customers who demand quantity as well as quality. The regulars include Lloyds Bank.

Bill has no hesitation in saying that the best Gun who has shot at Wintershall is National Car Parks boss Sir Donald Gosling, once a member of the syndicate there and now a regular taker of let days. 'He was the best tipper, too', said Bill, 'and always gave me £100 at Christmas. He even gives his loader £50. You could never be sure what you would get from some, and those full of promise would often disappoint. For example, my Christmas box from one noble syndicate member was just £20 – and that was a cheque! Of course, when there are a lot of let days and a constant stream of guests, keepers get much more than they do with a regular syndicate. And way back when I started and it was entirely an all-guest private shoot, the average tip was half-a-crown and the best 5s. In my last years the average was £10–£20 per Gun.'

Wintershall has seen a steady stream of famous and interesting guests. Prince Michael of Kent has been a guest of Sir Donald Gosling, and ex-syndicate regular Philip Darwin is the great-grandson of Charles Darwin, whose *Theory of Evolution* shocked Victorian society and set students of natural science in a new direction. Ironically, Philip Darwin is a good Shot so naturally concentrates on bagging the high-fliers, those good strong birds we all want, and therefore leaves a high proportion of weaker birds – a sort of reverse natural selection which would have given his great-grandfather plenty to puzzle over.

Another well-known guest was journalist and author Chapman Pincher. 'He was shooting next to Charles Hughesdon who kept shooting Chapman's birds and dropping them at his feet. After a while Chapman had had enough, so he marched over to Mr Hughesdon and said: "I knew you were going deaf, but not blind as well". But it was all good fun really and just one of the many amusing incidents which have made my days at Wintershall so enjoyable.'

Welcome refreshment in the field on Bill Gill's Wintershall shoot. Dispensing the beverages is Mrs Peter Hutley; crack Shot Sir Donald Gosling is front left

Bill still helps out on shoot days and often drives the game cart, thoroughly enjoying the company of the whole field, especially the loyal team of beaters, some of whom have shared Bill's good health over many years. In the old days Mrs Gill often had well over thirty beaters and loaders to lunch in their cottage.

'Some of those old boys were amazingly dedicated', Bill told me. 'I remember one Christmas – cor, it didn't half snow, and old Sir Keith offered the beaters an extra shilling each if they would turn out in the appalling conditions. Of course they went, and at dinner time things were so bad they had to pack in, but the boss still gave them their shilling.'

Today Bill and Gladys still live in their delightfully secluded semi-detached cottage, 'The Chestnuts', at Selhurst Common, where on some days there are as many horses as there are cars about the narrow lanes. The door is always open to a constant stream of true countrymen – those who know and respect Bill's love of the outdoors – and the delicious smell of home cooking drifts out over a real country garden, packed with big, bold flowers and immaculate rows of prize-winning vegetables which grace the harvest festival. In the shed are the many sticks which Bill expertly fashions from hedgerow trees such as holly, and in the house lie scattered mementoes of a lifetime's devotion to duty. Bill Gill may have called the shots for the last time at Wintershall, but he is still very much a bastion of Surrey's country scene.

Advertisement 1887

THE KEEPERS' BENEFIT SOCIETY

The object of the society is to provide for the widows or families of keepers who lose their lives in the protection of game, deer, or fish, also to provide with a yearly income those keepers who can produce a certificate from their present or late master, countersigned by a Justice of the Peace, that they are totally incapacitated from work on account of old age or accident. Such certificates must be renewed every six months. The word 'keeper' shall mean any person who is wholly employed in the protection of game, deer, or fish for sporting purposes.

Widows or families who come under the description given in Rule 1 will be entitled to receive £75 in a lump sum. After providing for these widows and families, and also for working expenses, the income of the society shall be divided annually in equal sums, not exceeding £25, among those benefit members who are totally incapacitated for work on account of old age or accident.

Minimum annual subscriptions of hon members £2 2s; life members' donations £26 5s; benefit members' annual subscription is 12s, and upwards, according to age.

No keeper over the age of 50 shall be allowed to join the society. All subscription of benefit members shall be paid for the whole of life, whether the member be in receipt of annuity or not.

The following scale of annual subscriptions will be adopted for all new benefit members:

Age	Annual Subscription £ s.	Age	Annual Subscription £ s.
Under 30	0 12	Under 40	1 6
30	0 13	41	1 7
31	0 14	42	1 9
32	0 16	43	1 11
33	0 17	44	1 13
34	0 18	45	1 15
35	1 0	46	1 18
36	1 1	47	2 1
37	1 2	48	2 5
38	1 3	49	2 9
39	1 4	50	2 14

Further details from the secretary, Mr George Arthur Battock at 4, Carlton Street, Regent Street, London.

Market Reports

London, 1 January 1895
J. Bridgman, Game Salesman, 203 and 205, West-end, Central Market, E.C.

Brace

Pheasants	6s 6d
Partridges (young)	4s 6d
Partridges (old)	2s 6d

Each			
Hares	3s 0d to 3s 9d	Rabbits (wild)	11d to 1s 2d
Leverets	2s 0d to 2s 6d	Surrey fowls	3s 6d to 5s 0d
Wild duck	2s 0d	Sussex fowls	3s 3d to 4s 0d
Pintail	1s 6d to 2s 0d	Lincolnshire fowls	2s 6d to 3s 6d
Widgeon	1s 2d	Essex fowls	2s 6d to 3s 6d
Teal	10d to 1s 0d	Irish fowls	2s 3d to 2s 9d
Golden plover	1s 0d to 1s 3d	Ducks	3s 0d to 4s 0d
Black plover	8d	Geese	5s 0d to 8s 0d
Snipe	1s 3d to 1s 6d	Turkeys (cocks)	8s 0d to 15s 0d
Woodcock	2s 6d to 3s 6d	Turkeys (hens)	5s 6d to 7s 0d
Rabbits (tame)	1s 3d to 1s 9d	Venison haunches (per lb)	15s to 18s
		Venison forequarters (per lb)	6d

The old game cart

Pot-hunting Keepers

As to keepers, there are very few of them, nowadays, who understand working dogs – let alone breaking them. A pot-hunting keeper is the worst possible man to have to break perfectly a retriever – because the man is so anxious not to lose a head of game that he will spoil a 40 guinea dog in order to secure a half-crown pheasant.

Lewis Clement in *Dog Breaking* (1880)

Concentration

Not Fast Enough

Despite being a former world-record motor-cyclist, poacher Maurice Egerton Davenport was not quick enough to evade capture by keepers in January 1938. But he certainly put up a struggle; his methods were likened by police to those of gangsters, and they regretted the fact that available punishment did not fit the crime.

Davenport was committed for trial at Macclesfield, Cheshire, accused of causing grievous bodily harm, 'casting a destructive fluid' at two keepers, being in possession of a weapon adapted for the discharge of a noxious gas and also using a firearm.

When chased by keepers, Davenport had suddenly turned round and flashed into their eyes a powerful torch, and twice discharged an irritant liquid onto the face of one keeper. In a hand-to-hand struggle with the other keeper, Davenport had bitten off part of the lobe of one ear. Expert evidence was that the fluid was benzine-bromide, which produced weeping and irritation of the nose and throat. It did not, however, have any permanent effect.

Police strongly opposed bail, but it was granted in three sureties of £500 each, on condition that Davenport reported to the local police station daily.

The Home Guard

While most keepers of 'army age' have joined the Colours, it is worthy of record that the very great majority of older keepers are serving with the Home Guard, where their knowledge of the local country, their natural abilities as 'woodcraftmen' and their understanding and expert use of firearms are proving of great value. Nor can it be denied that their judgement and advice, during field exercises, enjoys the confidence of those of high rank as well as that of the 'rank and file'. During their working hours – and there is no limit to the working hours of a keeper, especially in wartime! – these men not only serve the interests of the estates which employ them, but by doing so, in their capacity as vermin destroyers, also assist agriculture and the general war effort.

N. M. Sedgwick, *Shooting Times*, 1941

Mixing feed was a major task

Unusual Defence

A somewhat unusual defence was put forward in December 1923 when Albert Disney was charged with an offence under the Poaching Prevention Act – namely, that he was suspected of coming from land where he had been in search of game. The defendant had left Essendine by an early morning train – because it was suspected that he had been poaching, the railway officials at Grantham were notified and he was there met by the police, who found in his possession fourteen pheasants and a gun.

For the defence the facts were not disputed, but it was urged that it was not legal to search the defendant on a railway platform, which was private property. A case was mentioned where many years ago three Nottingham men had been convicted, but the High Court had quashed the conviction. For the prosecution it was pointed out that apparently there had been no actual judicial decision under the current statute, but the opinion was expressed in *Stone's Justices' Manual* that a railway station was a public place. As there were forty-one previous convictions against the prisoner, including seventeen for poaching, he was lucky to escape with a fine of two guineas and one guinea costs.

Death Fall

While firing at a flying hawk in the summer of 1932, gamekeeper M. Hutton of the Overtoun estate, Dumbarton, overbalanced and fell sixty feet from a ledge. He died from his injuries but the fate of the hawk is unknown.

Practised hands

A ferret for the keeper's son

Once a keeper, always a . . .

I fear that the sons of keepers are showing an increasing disposition to follow some calling other than that of their parent, and I can hardly wonder at this, as the remuneration is not such as to encourage them to adopt it. All the good old names seem to be disappearing from among the profession; at one time, all the most prominent positions were held by several keeper families. Some sons of their fathers remain keepers, but it is from sheer love of the outdoor life. Once a man becomes a gamekeeper he seldom tackles any other job. I knew one young fellow who was tempted to join the police, but he left when the shooting season arrived, and what do you imagine influenced him to do this? Nothing but the sight of the dead game appearing in the dealers' shop on his beat. This revived memories and longings he was quite unable to resist, and in a very short time he was a keeper again. Most young keepers start as kennel-boys and are at the beck and call of the staff, so they do not imbibe any misunderstanding as regards what they are in for. It is a suitable beginning.

'Hoverer', 1938

The Dangers of Copse Shooting

Driven shooting in cover has always demanded the highest standards of safety, particularly during the sport's early days when there was often less awareness of such matters. And very often it was the keeper who had to keep the peace. For example, in 1883 a gentleman cautiously enquired of the keeper: 'Who is that on my right?' 'Lord A, sir', replied that functionary. 'Just go and tell him where I am.' 'Beg pardon, sir, I'd rather not', said the keeper, touching his hat; 'his lordship always fires when he sees anything move!'

Terribly Unsporting Sir

A keeper was killed when a shooting party was fired upon from the German side of the Franco–German border in October 1887. At the same time an officer of dragoons was wounded terribly in the leg, necessitating amputation of the limb.

Not everyone was such a good shot

Feeding time

Trapped by a Footprint

Gamekeeper Joseph Looker of Woodstock Lodge, Ingatestone, Essex certainly displayed great initiative when he trapped a poacher in December 1887. As a result, labourer John Wright of Blackmoor was charged with stealing nine live, tame pheasants, value £4 10s, and remanded in custody.

When Looker had gone to his aviary on 18 December he had discovered that all his birds were gone. Someone had taken up the foundation under the brickwork and a hole had been made big enough for a man to get in. There were footmarks in the cage, and snow had been picked up on the boot of the person who had entered.

Looker had seen the prisoner and another man looking at the pheasantry a few days before. Subsequently, when police constable Lennon went to the house of Looker, he was shown a lump of snow, partly frozen, imprinted with the marks of the greater part of a boot. Using plaster of Paris, Lennon then took an impression of the footprint.

Later he apprehended Wright and seized his boot, the print of which matched that found a dozen yards from the aviary and was sufficient to secure a conviction.

Unwelcome intruder

Not one missed!

Climbing Keepers

Before the last war the average gamekeeper, whatever his age, was usually a courageous climber of trees and cliffs. In Wales, for example, some scaled cliffs to reach vermin nests on ledges, with efforts worthy of any practised Alpine climber, though they did not use any ropes or equipment.

As for trees, the keeper would shin up them with the agility of a monkey. But when trapping in nests became illegal keepers were not called upon to do so much climbing. Nonetheless, in the Thirties they still commonly climbed into the dense tops of evergreens as this was the only way they could see if vermin nests were present. Therefore many keepers possessed climbing irons, though there was some conflict with keen foresters who resented the tearing of the bark. Others managed to ascend by merely gripping with the knees, and for this a pair of tight-fitting corduroy breeches were useful.

Keepers also climbed very tall trees which were useful as observation posts, but they had to take special care with the larch for its boughs appear capable of bearing any reasonable weight but are treacherous enough to snap like glass.

Taking his chance

Boundary Bugbear

'The boundary is the bugbear of many a shoot', wrote A. A. Cousins in 1938. 'During the nesting season quite as many birds lay here as elsewhere. These eggs, in many cases, are picked up ruthlessly and placed elsewhere. Despite all this, good coveys manage to make their appearance and have an uncanny knack of 'this way and that' over the boundary fence. These birds are "no-man's birds" and sometimes lead to friction on the frontier. Do what you dare, they still remain "touch and go" targets for those on the fields across the way.'

The broody cost half-a-crown

Irish Humour

An instance of the humour which pervades even the magisterial bench in Ireland was apparent from the verdict in one of the cases appearing in the report of the Irish Game Protection Association in 1895. A man was charged with poaching and the law-givers ruled 'not guilty, but don't do it again!'

Rugby Tackle

Israel Buckle, who became headkeeper of Norfolk's Merton estate in 1835, was a small, active man renowned for his pluck and cleverness in catching poachers. On one occasion, when chasing a poacher along the furrow of a ploughed field, the man sloped his gun back over his shoulder and fired, blowing the brim off Buckle's hat. Buckle at once drove his head between the poacher's legs, and having upset him, sat on him until assistance arrived.

Times can be hard

The English Keeper Abroad

The English gamekeeper still seems to carry a reputation which men of other nationality in the same profession have never attained. Their services are in demand on the Continent and in America, and right well they prosper, despite no knowledge of the language in foreign countries. Some years ago I sent two gamekeepers to a Russian Grand Duke, and two years after their arrival the Revolution broke out and they suffered terribly. To save their lives they had to go, and they told me they trudged 400 miles before able to make train for the frontier, concealing themselves by day and walking only in the darkness. Murderous work was going on all the way. Fortunately all do not meet with such experiences, and some I know have remained abroad throughout their active lives, one especially, engaged in Austria, that land of game.

Thus wrote 'Hoverer' in *Shooting Times*, 1938. Fortunately, the British keeper is still very much in demand abroad, in America and many other countries, as the attractions of driven game spread across frontiers.

The Keeper's Inheritance

When Mr Vincent C. Stuart Wortley Corbett died, aged eighty-nine, on 26 November 1923, he left estate to the value of £47,036, and among his bequests were the following: to M. Harrison, gamekeeper, his guns (except his Purdey, which he left to his son-in-law) and rifles, his sporting dogs, and binoculars, and £100. His poultry, swans and black-and-white Muscovy ducks were left to his wife, and his fishing rods and tackle equally among his three sons-in-law.

Shooting 'Blind'

Back in the old muzzle-loading days Surrey gamekeeper Watts was known as a keen blade and a remarkably good Shot. When walking through thick fir plantations after pigeon he would fire the gun from the hip as soon as a half-visible bird fluttered among the boughs, and rarely was he unsuccessful. Only the muzzle would be raised from the position in which the gun was carried.

When rabbit shooting, Watts' experienced eye enabled him to detect the slightest movement and direction of 'buns', and guided by the merest trembling of the undergrowth he killed a rabbit for almost every shot without seeing the animal until he went to pick it up.

KEEPER WATTS AND SETTER.

'One-for-the-pot' man

Far from mad

Woodland sentry – the jay

Testing the air

FRANK HUNT

Nottinghamshire, Norfolk, Cheshire, Northamptonshire, Somerset, Kent and Surrey

The grandson of a poacher and son of a market-gardener, Frank ('Foxy') Hunt has keepered in seven counties, but, as his wife is quick to point out, 'we always left of our own accord and to better ourselves'.

Frank was born on 15 January 1908 at Collingham, near Newark, Nottingham-shire and his only experience of shooting before leaving school came through protecting the wheat on his father's allotment. 'The sparrows played hell with it so my father gave me an old muzzle-loader to shoot 'em.'

At the age of fourteen he was taken on as keeper's boy by Squire Curtis of Langford Hall, near Newark, the man who made his money through making gunpowder. He was also offered a job on the estate of Curtis' brother, on Tresco in the Scilly Isles, but his father said he was too young to go. So he stayed at home to mix feed, snare and bait traps for the squire.

After a year he went as keeper's boy for the Earl of Kimberley at North Walsham, on the Norfolk coast near Great Yarmouth, where he lodged with headkeeper Dawling. There he was put in charge of the donkey cart to take all the traps round – each keeper had ten dozen gins to look after. And he also had to take Mrs Dawling into North Walsham to do her shopping. 'She really fed me up on them there Norfolk dumplin's.'

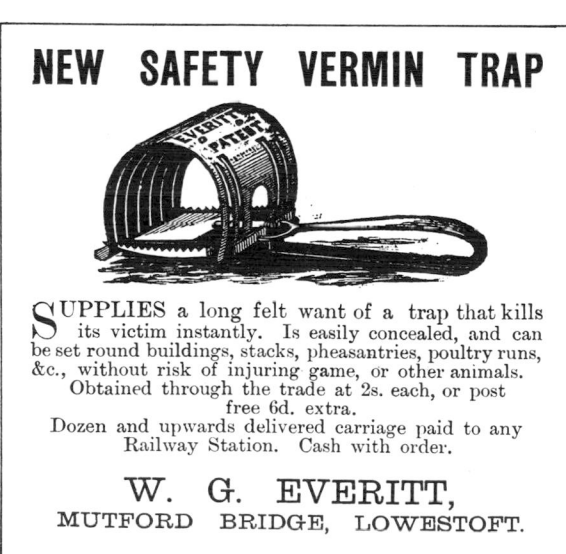

1887

Frank was paid £1 a week, but out of that he had to hand over 18s for board and lodging. Even so, on 2s spending money he managed to run a motorbike – a BSA 249, which his father loaned him £39 to buy. 'I remember going to visit my grandfather at Sleaford on it: quite an adventure in those days, and when I arrived safely at the farm everybody turned out to cheer.

'Our shoot was on pure sand and as a result there were thousands and thousands of rabbits there, so we was always ferretin'. We used a seven-foot spade with a hook on the end, and my job was to look after the ferrets and the dogs – curly coated retrievers. But I had to be careful where I deposited the ferret muck: the headkeeper told me – "You'll be doin' me garden too, but I can't stand ferret manure dug into it".

'I remember those days so clearly. It always seemed to be foggy and the nearby Happisburgh Lighthouse made a terrible din all night long. But it was a peaceful place, too, and it was a real pleasure to go motor cycling in those days.

'There was no industry in the area, though, and the only work was on the land. It was a hard life an' all. One day I met this poor old boy along the way and he said he'd walked five miles to do a day's thrashing, but when he arrived he got nothing because it was too wet to work and they were only paid by results. Those were the days of the reaper, engine and belt, before the binder.

'On shoot days I went about with the donkey cart gathering the shot game from places where the horse-drawn, main game cart was too heavy to go. There were seven keepers and they handled mostly partridges, but there were a few pheasants too.'

After five years in Norfolk, Frank went to work for Major Forbes at North Rode, near Congleton, Cheshire, where he assisted Jack Needham, who used to write for *The Gamekeeper*, in which the job was advertised. But it was rather strange how the vacancy arose, and all because at North Rode the mansion stood beside a big lake – the Guns would shoot pheasants up to lunchtime, and then turn their attention to the duck. But it was a long way round the lake so the single underkeeper had to row the Guns across the water to their shooting stations. Unfortunately, one day he tipped them all in and got the sack. So when Frank took his place he had to learn to become a good boatman too.

'In those days there was always someone knocking on the door trying to sell pheasant food, and the reps were always giving the keepers tickets to get them to visit their stands at Crufts. Lowes looked after us well, but Spratts always did us the best with a rare old meal – a knife and fork do, and they really pushed the boat out. The headkeepers always went to one side of the stand through a special entrance and were given whisky, while the underkeepers went round the other side and had to make do with beer.'

Crufts was the traditional clearing house for keepering jobs and it was well known that anyone standing near the Spratt's stand holding a white handkerchief or suchlike was waiting to be identified by a prospective employer.

It was while at North Rode that young Hunt started courting his future wife, Elizabeth ('Betty'), who worked in a cotton mill, wore clogs and shawl and had never been in the country in her life. Betty told me 'We met when we were on short time and with nothing else to do my friend and me decided to go for a walk into the country. We were really enjoying ourselves and got a nice bunch of

bluebells in the wood when all of a sudden someone came up behind us. "What the hell are you doin' here?" he bellowed. "And you can drop those", he said, staring at the bluebells we clutched nervously. "I have a lot of wild pheasants laying eggs here and I don't want anyone stompin' about breakin' 'em".

'But we wouldn't drop our flowers and the keeper ran us out of the wood. Then just as we were leaving he called out "I tell you what, I'll let you keep the flowers if you go out with me tonight". So I did, and that was how Frank and me began our life together.'

So, with a wife to support, Frank began to look for a better job, and he certainly came up trumps when he went to work as underkeeper for the extrovert Madame Sauber at Salcey Forest, between Newport Pagnell and Northampton. On this mixed shoot there was just one other keeper – the head – and the Hunts settled down happily in the ex-gardener's bothy in the rose garden.

When he attended for interview, Frank was met by Madame Sauber's chauffeur at the railway station. After a while they came to some big white gates and the chaffeur told Frank to jump out and open them. 'But when I did so he just whizzed past and left me standing, wondering what on earth was going on. Anyway, I followed him up the drive and eventually saw a lady sitting by some French windows. As soon as she saw me she let two awful terriers go at me. Trying to stay calm and stifle my anxiety, I put out my hand to the dogs and said, hopefully, "good boys". To my complete amazement and utter relief, they started wagging their tails.

'Then a high-pitched voice called out "Consider yourself engaged". The butler appeared like a statue by the kitchen door and declared "This way, please". He had a beautiful lunch waiting for me and while I was tucking in he started to interview me a bit. I even had a whole bottle of wine all to myself.

'Eventually, a bell rang, and the butler said "Madame will see you now". When I was ushered in, the first thing she said to me was "I expect you wondered why I said you were engaged when I hadn't even spoken to you. Well, I always engage my servants with those two dogs – John and Grouse. They always know an honest person – if they had bitten you I would have sent you back immediately".

'Then she asked me what money I wanted, so diplomatically I replied that she might care to suggest the amount. "All right, thirty shillings", she declared. "You will receive all your coal free and my head gardener will come round to your wife every morning to take her order for vegetables and fruit. A keeper hasn't the time to dig a garden." Thus began two years during which it seemed we couldn't do any wrong.

'Peacocks used to come and stand right in our doorway, and we had geese, guinea fowl, fancy pigeons and all sorts of birds to look after. We always had great big goose eggs for breakfast.

'Madame's husband was a German artist and their main house was in Knightsbridge. But they were both with us to shoot once a fortnight. She took such a liking to us she even left John and Grouse with us while she went to her villa in Monte Carlo. It was a great honour to be trusted so, but those dogs had to be really well looked after. They had a special cot each by our bed and every night we had to tuck them in with only their heads showing – just like babies. All the kennels were centrally heated and the butcher called every day to collect the kennelman's order.

'When she was home Madame used to send her lady's maid round to ask Mrs Hunt if she would like to go to the opera in Northampton. And we never refused anything in case we were never asked again. I was never invited on one of these jaunts, only Betty, but she loved them. However, we did go to local dances together. It was great fun rolling up to a sixpenny hop in a Rolls Royce!

'For my work they gave me a huge Harley-Davidson motorbike and sidecar as well as a Ford car for our own use – mostly for shopping in Northampton, where they had a really good market. We used to go late on a Saturday afternoon when they were auctioning everything off cheaply – you could get a great big lump of fish for sixpence and enough meat for a week for a shilling.

'On a shoot day the Guns came by train and we met them at the station. Everyone was extremely well looked after and there was even a special place for the dogs at lunch. Of course, with Madame's influence there were gallons and gallons of wine, and there was a great deal of whisky too. The bottles used to be stored in the coal shed after a weekend shoot and more than once I said "Bring the jug" as there was quite a bit left in some of the bottles. Mind you, Scotch was only 12s 6d a bottle then. Us keepers received more bottles than tips at Christmas.

'Talking about drink, I remember one day most distinctly. Madame had asked me to put a coop of pheasants on the lawn in front of the house so that she could enjoy watching the birds pecking about. But that night when I went to shut them up, I found her husband laid out on the lawn. When I went to pick him up she called out gruffly: "leave him there or you'll be out." They had obviously been drinking heavily and he was blind drunk. However, later on she came and asked me

to get him into the car as he had hit his head on the steps and needed medical attention.'

Life with Madame ended when Mrs Hunt became pregnant. There was 'no place for children there' and Frank was asked to consider looking for another position. So it was back to studying the 'Situations Vacant' columns in *The Gamekeeper*, and Frank soon secured a job as one of five beatkeepers on Lord Hylton's 15,000-acre (6,070ha) Ammerdown Park estate between Radstock and Frome. At the interview Frank was told the pay would be 35s a week, but he said that he had been offered other jobs and would not come for less than £2.

Lord Hylton had lost most of his interest in the shoot through a great personal tragedy. He always had a snooze in the afternoon and one day when he was sound asleep his son Toby took the gun cabinet keys from his pocket. The lad removed a shotgun and went off rabbit shooting with his sister; when they were passing the gun through a hedge it went off and Toby was killed outright.

After that the shoot was advertised and taken up by a group of men who saw the notice at their Bristol club. The wealthy syndicate included the tobacco family Wills and the jam-makers Robertson. But they had not been brought up to shoot in the tradition of landed gentry and needed to have coaching by Gibbs the gunmaker of Bristol. He used to come to stand behind them on a shoot. And as their enthusiasm increased, the keepers were required to rear more and more pheasants.

Then, after thirty years in the job, the headkeeper became ill and his doctor said he must retire. 'He was a big, fat chap', said Frank, 'and used to ride about in a pony and trap before he was pensioned off'.

Lord Hylton asked the head if there was anyone who could take over from him. 'Not really', he replied, 'there's only the "boy", but I could watch over him.' So next day Frank received a note, summoning him to see his lordship.

'He told me his son, Captain Jolliffe (that's the family name), was coming over and he wanted him to interview me for the position of headkeeper. Well, I nearly fell through the chair with complete surprise. Anyway, I saw the captain and he asked me to go with him as a loader on a two-day shoot at Lord Bath's. But long before we got to Longleat he had obviously made up his mind in the car and asked me to take over from headkeeper Sales. Some of the other keepers had been there for many years and you can imagine how surprised they were at my appointment. Anyway, after that I was a headkeeper for the rest of my working life.'

As headkeeper, Frank was paid £3 a week and given £6 10s a year clothes allowance. The underkeepers wore breeches but he donned knickerbockers and the tailor would come to his house to measure up.

'Each beat was expected to provide a day's shooting, and lunch was always held at the headkeeper's cottage. The butler would come down and when all the Guns had taken their fill we used to entice them into the sitting room as quickly as possible, by lighting the fire to make them nice and cosy, so that we could move in and feast on the left-overs!

Eighty-year-old Frank Hunt still has the old sieve through which they used to press hardboiled eggs in making the pheasant food

'About thirty local boys were employed as stops and they would all light fires to help keep the pheasants in. This also helped them to keep warm. They were all miners' sons and brought bags of coal along. Lunches were sent round to them along with jugs of hot cocoa, so they didn't go without. We had girls, too – and none of them seemed to mind the bitter winters we used to get.

'On the mantlepiece Betty kept a book and all the boys and girls used to come and enter their names in it, a couple of days before each shoot. Of course, they all wanted to earn a bit of pocket money and there was some competition among them. Sometimes they used to tease and suggest to each other that certain names were missing from the book. Then we would get irate fathers knocking on the door, wanting to know why young Johnny's name was not included.

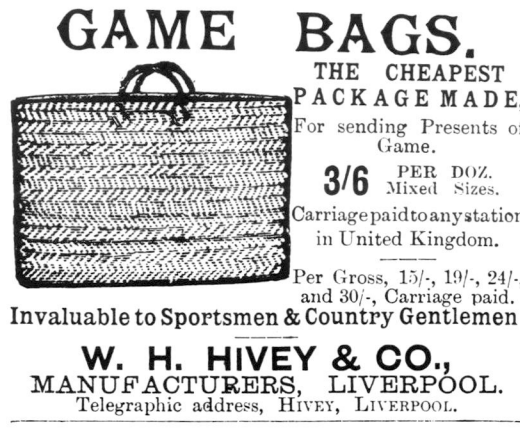

GAME BAGS.
THE CHEAPEST PACKAGE MADE,
For sending Presents of Game.

3/6 PER DOZ. Mixed Sizes.

Carriage paid to any station in United Kingdom.

Per Gross, 15/-, 19/-, 24/-, and 30/-, Carriage paid.

Invaluable to Sportsmen & Country Gentlemen

W. H. HIVEY & CO.,
MANUFACTURERS, LIVERPOOL.
Telegraphic address, HIVEY, LIVERPOOL.

1880's

'The children who did come received 2s 6d, a big lump of cheese, a pork pie and a bottle of pop, and the men beaters had 5s plus their lunch.

'Each beatkeeper was given five tons of coal a year, but, as headkeeper, I was given six even though I didn't need it. There was so much of it because it was produced on the estate and we never let our fires go out. When each new delivery came I gave what I had left over to the farmer up the road. We were supposed to pay the haulier but he never charged us. Anyway, we saw he was all right with a bird or two.

'My golly, didn't them ol' miners used to poach. We always had one down in the courts. They used to fight, too, but luckily I always seemed to come off best. And I joined up as a special constable to give me power over the roads. I was exempt from call-up because I was classified as a vermin destroyer.

'We had bombs dropped all over the estate when they missed Bristol. On one occasion her ladyship came out, complete with monocle, and said to me: "Weren't we lucky". But she didn't recognise me in my special's uniform directing the traffic. It was only when the shepherd accidentally let on that she twigged. And shortly afterwards his lordship marched up to me and said sharply: "I'll see you in the morning at 10am".

'Anyway, next day I duly reported to the office and his lordship said: "Do you get paid for that?" "Certainly not", I replied. And it was as well I didn't, as if I had he would certainly have cut my wages. But her ladyship was rather more sensitive and said to me: "My, you do look smart in your uniform, Mr Hunt".

'Of course, there was no rearing during the war with food rationed; then came one very sharp winter and I asked his lordship if I could buy a little corn for the birds. "Oh no", he said. "Let them die: there's a war on, don't you know." But we weren't too badly off as I knew a friendly farmer up the road.

'I used to kill a few birds for the market and they should have been sold at the controlled price of 9s for cocks and 8s for hens, but if someone didn't give me £2 a brace then I wouldn't deal with them again. They didn't have any choice really as meat was in such short supply and everyone wanted it. They even went mad for rabbits.

'Some people went mad when the Armistice was signed, too – they even tipped over the barrels which used to be kept along the road and set fire to the tar. Most people turned a blind eye, though.

'When his lordship died I was one of the chosen few to carry him to his grave in a horse-drawn farm wagon. The carter led the horse and four of us walked behind – me, the head gardener, the forester and the head carpenter, representing each department on the estate. The burial was at Kilminster, where his lordship used to pay the parson his living.

'Captain Jolliffe took over and I taught his two sons to shoot, just as I had already taught him. The syndicate was wound up and Captain Jolliffe took on all the shooting. His guests included Lord Bath, Major Duckworth and Lord Oxford of the Asquith family. Later Captain Jolliffe married Lady Perdita Asquith, daughter of the ex-Prime Minister. Asquith himself used to come to shoot and was quite a good

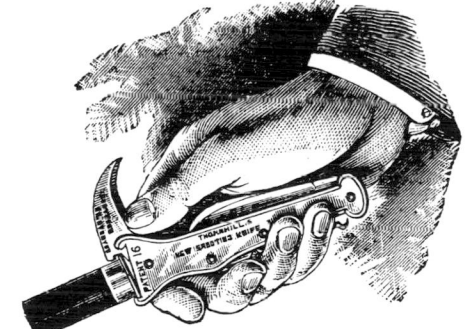

Shot. In those days we all had a saying: "You have to be like Asquith – wait and see".

'Despite mixing with the great and famous, Captain Jolliffe used to love going out, just us two, walking up the hedgerows to shoot a pheasant or two. And in September he liked to walk around after a few early partridges with me and his two boys, Raymond and John, before they went back to college. We had masses of partridges then as we grew so many roots.'

Frank was the only keeper left on the estate during the war. And when Lord Hylton died he was asked to go round with the valuers when they came to assess the estate, as he knew everyone so well and they all trusted him as a go-between. But it resulted in half a million to pay in death duties, so the shooting was cut back along with everything else and Frank's fourteen years on the estate drew to a close.

The butler asked Frank if he would like Lord Hylton's shooting clothes and he gladly accepted. 'What lovely tweeds and hand-knitted stockings they were: they lasted me for many years.'

Thus Frank went as a single-handed keeper for Mr Hussey at Scotney Castle, Kent, replacing an elderly keeper who was going to join his son in Australia. Hussey, the editor of *Country Life* magazine, was 'a very nice man who often came round to have a chat in our kitchen'.

One of the regulars at the Scotney Castle pheasant and duck shoot was Sir Robert McAlpine – 'another nice chap, though most of the guests were local Guns.

'I believe Hussey had been left the estate by his uncle. He was very particular about the view and hated to see any unnecessary buildings about. For example, there used to be a lot of hop-pickers' huts and he insisted that these were hidden away in the woods. And he opened the gardens to the public.'

Years later when Frank returned to look at the estate, he found his old shoot under water, sunk beneath a new reservoir, and he had to be shown round by the boatman on the pleasure lake! The castle had been turned into flats, one of which was taken by Margaret Thatcher. Frank again became a special constable when he moved to Kent and was made sergeant in charge of castle security.

Then Frank was recommended for another job by the Game Conservancy. Ockham Park at Ripley, near Guildford in Surrey, had become available through the death of Lord Lacey, who had died without heirs. The mansion had housed evacuees during the war and had become almost derelict, and the whole estate was very run down. Felix Fenston bought it, and wanted to establish a first-class shoot there – he had wanted his son to take over but tragically he had been killed in an air crash. Further land there was bought by Charles Hughesdon, who was to develop the shoot with Fenston.

When Frank took over the 2,000-acre (809ha) Ockham shoot there was only a lad to help him, yet they managed to put down some 2,000 pheasants plus 2,000 partridges.

Then Hughesdon sold his piece and the shoot became smaller; and its future seemed seriously in doubt when Fenston died, suddenly and unexpectedly, on the sleeper

After keepering in six other counties, Frank Hunt settled in Surrey, at Ockham Park

Frank Hunt outside his Surrey cottage in 1988

on his way to the shoot. The shoot did, however, carry on and a new syndicate was formed; it included Frank, who had free shooting in return for his work.

After a few years Mrs Fenston sent for Frank and told him she had decided to let Lord Forte have the shoot – apparently he already owned adjoining land and had been after the shoot for years as he thought it was taking his birds. But after just two years he gave it up, it was let to a builder and now it is overrun with vermin.

Frank gave up all involvement with the shoot in 1985. It was time to hang up his spurs. He had been a full-time keeper from the age of fourteen till he was seventy – fifty-six years, and even after that he was never far from the sound of guns. They had been 'happy as well as hard years' and he does not regret his chosen path. Now in their eighties, he and his wife have a quaint old cottage at Ockham Park where they can live for the rest of their days. Right on the busy main road, it is said to be the oldest house in Ripley, having previously been a pub and a police station.

On the day before I visited Frank, the eighty-year-old keeper had been knocked off his bike by a passing lorry, but luckily he was not injured. 'Now, if anyone wants me to help 'em out with their moles, rats, mice or bees they're going to have to fetch me.'

HARRY WARD

Blenheim (Oxfordshire) and Chawton (Hampshire)

Snug in her modern suburban home at Alton, Hampshire, Mrs Harry Ward clearly recalls the hard times of keepering life between the wars. 'We used to rely on the money Harry got for skins to buy all the little extras in life, and how well I remember holding the candle for him while he worked away into the night.'

Mrs Ward also vividly remembers how the Duchess of Marlborough used to come to their cottage on the Blenheim estate at Christmas with toys for the children. 'But Harry had to go up to see His Grace to collect his share of beef and baccy. And most of the time we never went anywhere, so when we were occasionally taken in a bus to a Marlborough family event, such as a twenty-first birthday party, it was a real treat.'

But despite the hardships, Harry did not hesitate in telling me that he 'would do it all again', adding, as he turned to his wife, 'After all, it never killed us, did it?' Their children were always very involved in the keepering life and spent many happy hours out on the rearing field with them. However, although his son is now a single-handed keeper at New Milton, Hampshire, Harry would advise most men not to take up keepering today.

Born in prime shooting country, at Deopham, Norfolk on 9 June 1909, Harry got his first job through the Gamekeepers' Association. At the age of fifteen he followed in his grandfather's (but not his father's) footsteps by joining the profession as kennel boy for the excellent mixed shoot run by a syndicate at Nateby, Lancashire, where he earned 16s a week.

After this customary apprenticeship, Harry went as underkeeper to Lord Portman's at Orchard Portman, near Taunton, Somerset, and from there to Hollington, near Newbury for three years as underkeeper for Mr Eliot Cohen.

In 1931 Harry moved again, this time to prestigious Blenheim, where his promotion to beatkeeper was a great spur to settling down – this was the year in which he married. He was to stay there for sixteen years, though from 1940 to 1945 he was with the 117 Regiment, mainly on heavy ack-ack duties in England.

At first, Harry worked for the ninth Duke of Marlborough, a little man generally known as 'Sonny', who 'liked to be called "Your Grace".' In fact this became quite a joke among all the employees, some of whom impudently used the words 'Your Grace' with unnecessary frequency when addressing their master.

Under Sonny, the keepers' uniform remained very traditional – 'If it was good enough for my father then it's good enough for me', he said on several occasions. So the bowler hats and button-backed coats remained till Sonny's son took over.

Harry recalls that Sonny was a reasonable Shot but 'Lord Carnarvon was less hurried and a nicer Shot altogether'. In fact, it appears that Carnarvon never really liked Sonny, for in his memoirs he wrote:

Sonny was a pompous little man and I remember one Boxing Day, just as we were finishing breakfast and looking forward to a day's shooting, the butler came in and said, somewhat nervously, 'Your Grace, I have a message from your headkeeper to say that he is ill and will not be able to come out shooting today. He wishes to assure Your Grace that he has delegated all his responsibilities to the keeper on the beat and he hopes you will have a good day'. Sonny listened in chilly silence which communicated itself to all the guests. He replied: 'My compliments to my headkeeper; will you please inform him that the lower orders are *never* ill'.

In the early years at Blenheim every one hundred coops would produce about 1,500 pheasants in a good season, but 'there was round-the-clock work for every man'. And Mrs Ward recalls that when they were first married they used to go nightwatching together. 'I was too scared to stay in the house alone and used to sleep on a few sacks while he stood guard.'

Also etched in Mrs Ward's mind is the day Sonny was brought back to Blenheim for burial. 'Of course, all the keepers had to be on parade, and what polishing of boots went on that morning!'

Sonny was succeeded by John, the tenth duke, generally known as Bert, and according to Harry 'he was as tall as his father was short'. He was an excellent Shot, but renowned for putting himself in all the best positions. 'For example, as you know, few people are keen to take their turn as walking Gun, and many were most grateful when Bert offered to take their place. But the thing is, we keepers knew that Bert only suggested this when he knew good sport would come his way.

'Bert expected everything to be just so, often quite unreasonably. For example, the way he used to say "hurry up" to his loader Bill Monks, who was the fastest loader I ever saw. Bill was also the Duke's valet, and always drank a pint of beer before breakfast.'

Among other distinguished guests, Harry clearly remembers Winston Churchill, Sonny's cousin. 'He was not really very keen on shooting and always preferred

Harry Ward received his first long-service award in 1976. 'Prince Charles was very kind to me'

CONSIDERATE MASTERS

informal days, sometimes on his own. Even then he rapidly grew tired of it and would soon go off painting for an hour or two.'

When Harry first went to Blenheim the beaters were given sandwiches for lunch, but later this was done away with and instead they were given 2s, because of the rationing. 'The keepers and loaders always had soup and Irish stew plus a bottle of light or dark ale, but you had to be quick to get a bottle of brown. And while we joked and ate, the Guns always went to the Palace for lunch.'

The Blenheim headkeeper always shared out the tips at the end of the season, as was customary. 'And he was very fair in sharing out the paid jobs as loader or picker-up on neighbouring estates.'

In 1947 Harry went to Chawton in Hampshire, as beatkeeper for Edward Knight, but the shoot was very run down. However, in 1954 the estate was bought by Major Richard Sharples and 45-year-old Harry at last became headkeeper.

Sharples was to be Harry's favourite employer – 'A real toff: quite unlike His Grace, who always wanted you to touch your hat too much.' Later he became Sir Richard Sharples and Governor of Bermuda; a tragic appointment because he was assassinated over there.

Lady Sharples became Harry's employer and later she married Patrick de Lazslo. When he died, Harry worked for his son Damon until retiring in July 1987 (part-time from 1965). That was the month in which Harry received his Country Landowners Association award for forty years on one estate. He had already received the CLA medal for forty years on two estates when the Game Fair was held in Wales in 1976: 'It rained most of the day, but Prince Charles was very kind to me and set me at my ease.'

No sluggard even in retirement, Harry aims to 'make up for lost time': he is a very keen golfer and shares with his wife a keen interest in cage-birds. The hard years are long behind them now, but as the dust settles on the medals and family snapshots of friends long gone, the memory of it all remains as crisp as ever.

Note: Sadly, Harry Ward died in 1992, aged 82.

The Keeper's Pleasures

The gamekeeper has no use for the Eight Hours Act, or any other so far as his time is concerned, as there is not one of the twenty-four in which his presence may not be required, as the resting and leisure time of other people is his busiest time, he having to be on the lookout for possible marauders, and the Summer Time Act has been anything but a blessing to him, giving as it does more time for wrong-doing to those so inclined, and his life is not at all a bed of roses. His work is of a very arduous nature, still it is full of compensations and pleasures to a real lover of sport and companionship of wild nature. If he is an intelligent man and desirous of reading that book, it is open to him daily. He knows and notes the heralds of each season as it comes through the agency of the different things he sees and hears daily in his travels. He learns, and knows the meaning of, many things of which the town dweller or sedentary worker has no conception. Going his rounds he sees where a fox has made his spring upon a rabbit, or taken a sitting pheasant or partridge from her nest. A circle of feathers from a bird will tell him that a sparrowhaw has made its kill or poachers have been netting, and he will be able to decide which has been the culprit. A rabbit's skin cleanly taken off and the carcase consumed, a rabbit's nest with a perpendicular hole down to it, or a wasps' nest cleaned out the same way, shows that a badger has been at work.

A dead rabbit with a small hole in its neck marks the presence of a stoat. A young pheasant without its head tells him that he has an especially vicious owl in his coverts which, if not captured, will deplete his stock more than can be endured. Young pheasants about the coops may be found dead, and only the brain gone, and he knows that a jackdaw has paid him a visit. The warning notes of the smaller birds indicate to him the presence of a foe, and the particular note will tell him if it is furred or feathered enemy they have detected. He knows that when rabbits appear from their burrows to feed much earlier than usual they are taking advantage of the weather to prepare for the enforced want of food owing to stormy weather

The stoat was much commoner

approaching, and that the same weather wisdom is possessed by rooks and other birds and animals.

During his lonely vigils at night, sitting in the lee of a hedge, or in a wood, he hears the dog fox calling to his mate, and her answering shriek; the whistle of the otter and others of the midnight wanderers, and can distinguish them all. The song of the nightingale in the south and the hedge-sparrow in the north is sweet music, and on the other hand, probably the most eerie of all the sounds he hears will be a fight between two hedgehogs, which can most nearly be compared to the dying moans of a little child.

The first and each succeeding fall of snow is eagerly looked for by the keeper as it leaves the tell-tale footprints of ground vermin, and he is able to see what there is upon his beat. Taking his gun and two or three traps in his gamebag he will search for signs of them, and when found, follow till he gets where they are, probably in a rabbit burrow, an old covered-in drain, or a stack bottom. Should it be a stoat or weasel, he will imitate the dying shrieks of a rabbit, which, if the animal has not had a kill just previously, will draw the culprit to the sound and its own death. If this is not successful a trap can be set, which is sure to do its work, particularly if the table has been smeared with a few drops of blood. It is always advisable to take a ferret also, for if a stoat or weasel has been disturbed, they may not look out of their harbour, and it may be difficult to trap, but if the ferret is turned down after them they will bolt at once. This can also be done with a fox, providing he has not been run by hounds, and everything kept quiet. A colony of rats may be located, which had escaped notice before, and the burrows most favoured by rabbits noted.

Head and single-handed keepers generally have game licences taken out by their employers to enable them to replenish the larder when required, and when that has to be done, a conscientious man will always tramp his boundary, or some other place his employer does not care to walk over, thus leaving the better and easier part of the shoot for his employer and his party. It is quite in order that the keeper should have this licence, and for the good of the preserve in that he can pick off surplus cock partridges or old cock pheasants that are leading his young hand-reared birds away from home in October.

To the moorland keeper it is especially useful, as he is able to bag a few old cock grouse that dominate more ground than they should by being upon the moor

During the war the rat ran riot

131

before daylight and using a clay pipe in imitating the call of the female grouse, and this is a very killing method on a sharp, frosty morning.

In some districts in pre-war days it was the custom of the owner of the shoot to give a party of adjoining keepers a day amongst the cock pheasants at the end of the season, and this was eagerly looked forward to by those invited. A full staff of beaters was engaged, hot lunch set out for all, and a dinner at night for the keepers, to be followed by a smoking concert and a brace of pheasants each to take home marked a most enjoyable day. There was almost sure to be some of the gentlemen who shot the estate following to see the shooting and chaff the unfortunate keeper who missed a sitter, though in general the shooting was quite up to their average.

The moorland keeper obtains much more shooting than his lowland brother, and particularly if he is good at driven birds, and when game is plentiful he is pretty constantly engaged towards the end of the season supplying his master, who may live a considerable distance away. Also when inclement weather may be expected and fireside sportsmen shun the ordeal he has many an invitation to assist, and very probably his contribution to the bag will be the largest.

As time rolls on and he feels unfit for his duties, and rheumatism, the result of the many soakings he has had, assails him, he may, if he has been a steady, thrifty man, held good situations, and had good luck, rent a small farm or hotel, or be retained upon the estate in light employment as a trusty servant, and if he has been serving one of the old county families or local squires, will almost certainly receive a pension which, if he has a little of his own, may enable him to end his days upon the place, and amongst the game he has protected so long, and the scenes of his former achievements, and he will always be pleased to give his matured advice to those who have taken up his duties, and this will be well worthy of acceptance.

J. Parker, 1931

Is the keeper coming?

'We had to know every number plate'

Killed by a Christian

'I shot to prevent Wright from shooting me. I had to do it in self-defence. It was the only thing to do.' This was the defence of Claude Christian, a gamekeeper of Hooton Roberts, charged at Doncaster in 1932 with causing the death of Charles Wright of Denaby, by shooting him.

Police Sergeant Waugh said that on the afternoon of 15 March 1932 Christian had run into his station at Conisborough in a very excited state and said: 'I have shot him. There were four of them poaching in Denaby Wood. Two of them threatened me with a gun. I had to do it. Come on, quick.'

They went to the scene of the alleged shooting but found nobody there. The officer said that Wright was an habitual poacher but did not know if the deceased regularly carried firearms, though he knew he readily resorted to violence.

Christian said that when he first saw the four men in the wood they were working like an ordinary shooting party. Two men with guns were on the outside and two men with sticks in the middle. Wright had said: 'You – off! I know how far your beat goes.'

As Christian followed them Wright had said: 'Let's settle him. I've shot . . .s like him in France. I'll do it again.' Christian told the court: 'When we got further on, Wright had his gun out and brought it to his shoulder. I have no doubt that at the time Wright was taking aim at me and that he was about to shoot me. So I fired my gun from my hip, and at the same time jumped on one side, thinking he might pull his trigger first.'

After a short retirement, the magistrates announced that this was not a case which should go before a jury, and dismissed it.

Situations Wanted and Vacant

From *Shooting Times and British Sportsman*, 5 January 1895.

CAN any gentleman thoroughly recommend gamekeeper, head of 3 or 4. A sober, honest, industrious and competent man. Particulars and wages to Hamilton Fletcher Esq, Brookwood Park, Alresford, Hants.

J. FROOME, headkeeper, Ellisfield, Basingstoke, wishes to recommend his second man as gamekeeper, single-handed or good beat. Well up in all his duties. Honest, sober and trustworthy. Age 24. Height 6 feet. Weight 13 stone. Would get married when suited. Leaving through shooting given up.

GAMEKEEPER (under or beat); married man, age 42; eight years' character; good rabbit and vermin catcher; strong and active. Col. H. Barclay, Tingrith Manor, Woburn, Beds.

A GENTLEMAN wishes to recommend his keeper; age 36; weight 13st. 7lb; married; small family; thoroughly understands rearing and charge of game, foxes etc; not above making himself generally useful, and has had considerable experience with cattle; a reliable, trustworthy servant. Address W., Pear Tree House, Great Horwood, Bucks.

The old campaigner

The Yolks on Her

In 1928 a keeper met a woman leaving one of his coverts and felt certain that pheasants' eggs were hidden on her person. He was in a quandary as to what was best to do under the circumstances, when a brilliant idea struck him. He greeted her cheerily and stepped along by her side till they both arrived at a gate, which he politely opened for her. When the lady was halfway through he slammed the gate against her skirts and the yolks of the eggs came pouring down on her feet. A female searcher at the police station found her wearing a petticoat fitted inside with rows of little pockets, each of which contained an egg. She was conveying away a lot of eggs collected and cached by someone else.

In those days women were useful to poachers in many other ways, though few actually poached. For example, they acted as spies when calling at a keeper's house under the pretext of having a basket of odds and ends for sale.

Women were also used for carrying poaching equipment to the intended scene of operations, though this was much easier in the days when voluminous dresses were worn, easily concealing snares, nets etc.

Then there was the innocent-looking courting couple sitting on the stile, apparently engrossed in each other but really taking a note of where coveys settled down for the night, preparatory to a netting raid.

At other times women were used for picking up poached game from where it had been dumped, and getting it home or to market. The innocent bundle of sticks, wrapped in a piece of sacking, which once a woman might have carried on her head, would hide quite a lot of game, and much more would rest beneath a baby in a perambulator – the keeper was always wary of a pram in which the baby rode unusually high. In one case a woman was stopped with a heavily loaded baby carriage which she asserted contained fowls she was selling from her own stock. Each bird was plucked and neatly trussed, and the constable who stopped her was nonplussed till he examined the birds and discovered shot holes.

Dastardly Disney

When Belvoir estate underkeeper Joseph Geeson and a colleague chased poacher Albert Disney on 9 February 1932 they did not realise what a hard man they were up against. Geeson and two other keepers went to Anneses Gorse when they heard shots. They saw two men leave, and Geeson and his brother pursued one. But when they caught up with the man and flashed a light in his face, he said: 'Stand back or I'll blow your brains out'. However, as the poacher pointed the gun at them Geeson immediately struck him on the arm with his stick. Disney fell down and as he did so the gun fired into the ground.

At Melton Police Court the South Nottingham labourer pleaded guilty and admitted poaching for pheasants. Superintendent Smith said that between 1896 and that date Disney had been convicted sixty-one times, including various poaching offences, and once for wounding with intent to do grievous bodily harm. For this night-poaching offence at Sproxton he was sentenced to six months hard labour.

A Bloody Confrontation

In the past, gamekeepers very often met violence with violence, and a good example of this came to court in February 1932. Major Miller-Munday's keeper Edward Lister was cycling along Fullerton Road, Red Rice when he heard shots. He rode on to the plantation and saw Arthur Bowley of Andover coming out of the belt. Lister asked Bowley what game he was at, whereupon Bowley ran away. But the keeper soon overtook the poacher and closed in on him. There was a struggle and Lister struck Bowley with a piece of wood. They then went together for about a hundred yards before Bowley struggled again. He took off his coat, threw it down in front of Lister, tripped him up, and then ran away in the darkness. There were six pheasants in the coat.

P. S. Wren said that Bowley admitted that he had gone to Red Rice, taken his gun, killed several pheasants and put them in the lining of his coat. Bowley told the court he had been out of work for ten weeks, and as he was getting only 25s a

The stand marker

week they could not manage on it, with 7s a week rent to pay. Lister had hit him on the back of the neck, dragged him along, and his collar and clothing were soaked with blood through the bruising he had received.

Supt Bennett said Bowley had been convicted previously for trespassing in search of game. Bowley was fined £1 in each case and the gun was confiscated. A month was allowed in which to pay the money.

The Sheikh's Loader

In the 1970s an Arab sheikh was so delighted when told that his bag of Longleat pheasants was the best of the day he rewarded his loader with £1,000 and gold jewellery. The truth is that his loader, Patrick Fletcher, a part-time keeper, had been 'cleaning up' behind him, and the real 'score' was Sheikh 1, Fletcher 24.

The only means of transport

Too Hot for Comfort

On one occasion when gundog handler Bill Meldrum (now Sandringham's headkeeper) accompanied Her Majesty Queen Elizabeth to Broadlands, the Hampshire home of Lord Romsey, he found the heat of the house too much to bear. Rising in the night to open his bedroom window, he unfortunately set all the alarms off, and instantly the grounds were full of highly attentive emergency services fearful for Her Majesty's wellbeing. Apparently red-faced Bill should have opened his window *before* the alarms were set.

Plenty of lead

The Keeper's Vote

A Victorian politician, who made a point of canvassing wherever he went, solicited the vote of the headkeeper where he was shooting, for the local Conservative candidate. The following dialogue took place.

Keeper: 'Well, sir, I be going to vote for Mr . . . (the Conservative candidate) and so be all my mates.'

Canvasser: 'Quite right. Mr . . . is pledged to support Lord Salisbury and his foreign policy is . . .'

'Lord, sir', interrupted the keeper, 'we don't know nothing about no foreign policy; it was because they passed that . . . Ground Game Act we won't vote for t'other party.'

Vigorous in Old Age

It is astonishing how vigorous gamekeepers remain during old age. I know of one or two still holding their positions although well over the allotted span; they are upright and lissom. The bane of the keeper is too often rheumatism, because he is careless in protecting himself in bad weather and given to kneeling on the bare earth when trapping. Many succumb to this as the years advance and live to regret the follies of youth. I am acquainted with several old keepers enjoying a pensioned existence on the estates they so long looked after, and dear old chaps they are, full of anecdote and reminiscence. It is astonishing how loyal they are to their younger successors and that jealousy does not divide. In these days pensions seldom come the keeper's way, for leases of shoots too often are short and syndicates forget good service, even if in a position to acknowledge it. Few keepers are now able to put by a competence, for tips are not what they were and the cost of living has increased.

'Hoverer', 1938

The Keeper's Cottage.

'Royal' Poacher's Success

The following anecdote relates a case in which the poachers scored: a noted deer poacher made a grand shot at a great 'royal' stag, but unfortunately the keepers were spying this beast at the very moment that it staggered and fell. It must have been a long shot, for not a sign of the poacher could be seen; the only thing that could be done was for the two keepers to stalk the poacher if they could find out his whereabouts and the other two to watch, in the meantime, to see him come to the beast.

Neither the men with the telescope nor the others got a glimpse of the poacher at all that day, and all were prevented by the head stalker from going near the dead beast in case the poacher was spying.

When it was getting dark the keepers held a council of war, and they agreed that the poacher only wanted the head of the big beast, and would very likely come to get it at about ten or eleven that night, after the moon was up. Opinions were divided as to whether the poacher had 'smelt a rat' or not, but it was agreed that all four should lie behind the stag, two at it and two on the most practicable road to it.

It was a fine moonlit night but very cold, and the keepers were nearly frozen when the poacher appeared walking on the steep slope of the hill, and keeping well clear of all rocks. He made no attempt to come near the stag, but from a point on the steep hillside began to throw and roll stones at the carcass.

The two keepers behind the carcass stood the bombardment well, but at last one of them was hit by a stone, and could not help giving a groan: so the game was up, and all four keepers joined in a fruitless chase of the poacher, whom they followed for miles, but finally lost completely.

Slowly and sadly they returned to the dead stag to make spoil of its head, but were surprised to find it gone. The whole thing had been a 'plant' of course, for afterwards it became known that the poacher had seen the keepers before he shot the stag, and had planned every detail for the recovery of his booty, even to the extent of having confederates in waiting with a pony, while he lured the keepers away in pursuit of himself.

Mark of the Poacher

Several keepers recall how in the old days they would watch for markers which were left by poachers to assist them in their night-time raids. Their favourite was a piece of broken white crockery, which is visible however dark the night and reflects any light there happens to be.

The poachers used to go over a field and place a piece of crockery by each bush, as a means of avoiding them when dragging a net. In the same way, rabbit holes and smeuses used by hares through fences were marked, which must have been a great help to those setting snares or ferreting by night. Nor was it unknown for a farm worker, actually in alliance with poachers, to·walk along a fence apparently eating a turnip – he was in fact being careful to drop a slice close by each smeuse. But a slice of this root does not remain white for very long so, if seen fresh, an attempt at poaching could be anticipated very soon after.

Feeding the ferrets

Getting the Brush Off

In the summer of 1924 a keeper was on his way towards a clearing in a wood where some of his pheasant pens were situated. Suddenly a loud cackling broke forth from the penned birds, followed by a piercing screeching like that of a fowl about to have its neck wrung. Hurrying to the spot through the trees, his feet making little sound on the carpet of pine needles, the keeper arrived in time to witness a curious sight.

Outside one of the pens was a fox, and it was making grabs at one of the hens inside. Her mother love roused by the danger to her chicks, the hen was making darts at Reynard's mask between the bars of the pen, uttering her strident cries the while. The fox, of course, could not get his jaws through the bars, neither was it quick enough to snatch the bird's head when it poked out. The noise effectively drowned all sound of the keeper's approach, so that he was able to get right behind the animal and catch hold of its brush. The man's anger at seeing his precious charges in peril was such that he forgot the sacred character of the marauder, and, whirling it round and round, he looked about for a tree on which to dash its brains. But ere he could do this the brush, wet with dew, slipped out of his grasp and the fox was free.

Cider and beer enough for all

Full of Good Ale

Joseph Man, born at Poles Walden, Hertfordshire in the early years of the eighteenth century, had a quaint fringe of white hair which gave him a venerable appearance indicative of more advanced years. It is recorded that a severe attack of fever at nineteen years of age turned his hair white in a single night.

Joseph was probably rather proud of his prematurely bleached head covering; no doubt it invested him with considerable interest in the eyes of his neighbours. The patriarchal appearance of this noted gamekeeper earned for him quite early in life the appellation 'Old Joe Man' or 'Daddy'.

He was evidently a faithful and valued servant, having spent forty-four years in the service of the Viscount Torringtons as huntsman–gamekeeper. Joe was reputed to be an expert on shooting methods, game preserving and the hunting of hares.

Joe Man attributed his long working life to his consistent habit of never going to bed until he was full of good ale; a habit, he averred, that would never harm anyone who was an early riser and a follower of fieldsports. Whatever anyone thinks of that, the fact remains that Joe was able to get about with a gun until he died at eighty-one years of age.

Lamb to the Slaughter

When keepers on the Glensaug were out looking for foxes in the Slough of the Birnic, near Clatterin' Brigs, in April 1895, they observed a golden eagle rise from a rock nearby. Assistant keeper John Templeton fired, and brought down the bird. It was 'in splendid condition and measured seven feet from tip to tip'. When disturbed the eagle was making a substantial meal of a lamb about ten days old. As there were no lambs within at least a mile and a half of the place where the eagle was, the keepers assumed the eagle must have carried its prey a considerable distance. But could a fox have taken it there?

Peculiar Gun Accident

A most unfortunate accident took place at Kirkintilloch on New Year's Day, 1895. George Pollock, of Milton, was coming to Kirkintilloch when he was met by Alexander Scobbie, a man repeatedly convicted of poaching. There were one or two others present and Scobbie had been asking them to stand treat, when his gun dropped from inside his coat: the charge went off and completely smashed Pollock's right foot.

The hare was very common

And Uncle Tom Cobley An' All

Thomas Cobley was one of four Barwell labourers charged by Leicestershire keeper Frank Maidment with trespassing in search of game or conies on the land of Joseph Bonset at Elmsthorpe on 10 April 1887.

Charles Webb, woodman, said that at about 4pm he was inside the plantation at Burbage Wood when he heard a noise like someone beating the hedge. Subsequently he saw Charles Buckby doing just that, and Tom Cobley went through the hedge onto adjoining land. John Astley and Sandford Herbert were in the lane, telling the other two when a rabbit ran in and out of the fence. Eventually their dog caught a rabbit.

Herbert could not be positively identified and the case against him was dropped, but the other three were each fined 20s and costs, or in default fourteen days hard labour. There were previous convictions against all of them.

AMATEUR POACHING.

HARRY CHURCHILL
Dorset and Northamptonshire

Even Thomas Hardy would have enthused over the unspoilt corner of Dorset where Harry Churchill spent his childhood and discovered the profession which made his family famous. But the country lad who turned his back on book learning and preferred to study the ways of fox and pheasant never dreamed that he would become a TV star in his seventies!

Henry Frank Churchill was born on 7 December 1907 in the tiny village of Turnworth, near Blandford Forum, where his father was keeper to Colonel Parry-Ogden – 'he of the expensive complexion, with a great big red-and-purple nose which was said to be the result of a dog bite'.

Keepering was certainly in the family blood as Harry's grandfather and great-grandfather were keepers, too, as were his father's four brothers, and Harry himself was one of five brothers, four of whom took up the profession.

Harry's first experience of shooting came at the tender age of five, when his father took him to the edge of a wood close to a chalkpit and said: 'You stay here till you're fetched and don't you move'. He was also told that someone would bring him lunch, which consisted of 'half a loaf with a chunk cut out the middle and a lump of butter stuffed inside, and a bottle of lemonade, of course'.

After lunch Harry was moved, but still had no idea of what he was supposed to be doing, and it was years later before he realised that he had been posted as a 'stop' to dissuade birds from running out the sides of drives. 'I can still see those birds coming over, but the only way I could have stopped them there was with a 12-bore – certainly not my hands. Yet in many situations a kid is as good as an older man.'

Also that year came Harry's first experience of foxhunting. 'Our house was on the edge of a big wood, where the hounds came drawing through one day. I remember how frightened I was because their tongues were hanging out and I really thought they were going to gobble me up: all quite unnerving and larger than life for a toddler.'

Another vivid memory of dogs from childhood concerned a lurcher belonging to a Scots farmer called Maitland, who had land on the beat of Harry's father. 'One day that ravenous dog caught a big rabbit and brought it back to the feet of my brother and me. How utterly amazed I was as the dog proceeded to eat the entire rabbit, beginning with the head.'

Happier recollections involved the rearing field hut, where the young Churchill would perch on the food sacks listening to the keepers' wondrous tales during their rare moments of rest. He can remember seeing the food boiler full of hens' eggs, 'imported from Poland of all places. The underkeepers used to give us kids a few to

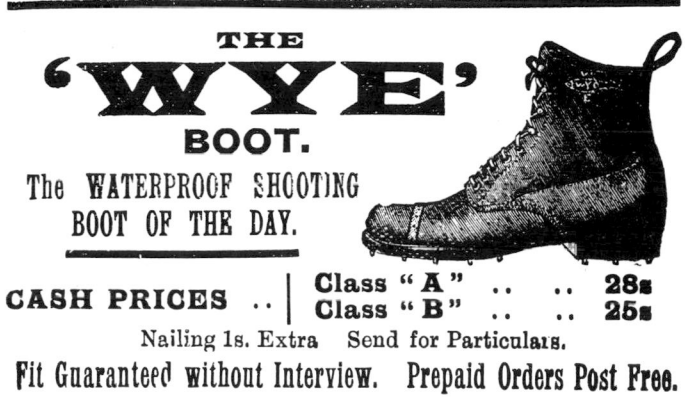

eat on the way home, as well as handfuls of the scalded biscuit meal meant for the birds.

'The pheasants were always started off on sieved eggs dusted with powder – very fine barley meal and a spiced concoction from Spratt's to make it more palatable.

'I detested school in those days and would always rather be off birdsnesting. Not surprisingly, I was always either in the classroom corner with hands on head, or off somewhere. You could be certain that whenever the hounds came round I was off to watch, and I had a good trick to skive off, too – I took bread and marge to school for lunch, and I would chew some up, then spit it out and pretend to be sick. But instead of going home I was straight off hunting.

'I also skived off to go beating. In fact I did it so often that when I went into school the next morning I would sometimes hold out my hand and say "You might as well cane me now". It was a hazel rod they used on me, and the girl who wielded it – Alice Chamberlain – died only a couple of years ago.

Harry's father also worked as a beatkeeper for Lord Eustace Cecil at Lytchett Matravers, Dorset, but left there in 1914 to go back to Turnworth, as a single-handed keeper, after he was declared too old for military service. The war had already started when the family made their adventurous return by double-shaft wagon pulled by two horses.

'Mr Carter, the carter, came and stayed the night and loaded up our few possessions. Our old settee was perched right on the front of the cart and the whole family sat on it, all in a row. On our way we stopped at the Chequers pub, and mum and dad went in while us kids stayed put, but they did bring us out one of those large biscuits each, of the kind you could buy anywhere at the time.

The cottage at Turnworth was on the second-highest point in Dorset, and we had to fetch more horses to get us up the hill. The farmer who helped us had a Jersey herd which produced the most wonderful yellow butter you ever saw. We must have eaten pounds of it between us, with slice after slice of bread. We were all so hungry that day and must have made real pigs of ourselves.

'We were pretty remote at Turnworth and often cut off by snowdrifts. The only thing delivered was a sack of flour brought in by donkey and cart. Mother used to walk seven miles to get the groceries. She used to make such wonderful bread in an oven in the wall. I can still see her now, punching the dough in a big earthenware pot before setting it near the fire to rise. She had a long, flat board to pop the loaves in the oven, and she also made marvellous lardy cakes: you can't buy the like of 'em now. And us kids had to fetch the wood to fire the oven till it was white-hot. What a thirst we used to work up, but there was always a glass of goat's milk available; in fact we were brought up on it.

'It was a wonderful place where we lived, and on a clear day we could see five counties and the Isle of Wight from the cottage. Now our old home near Bulbarrow viewpoint, Ringmore is just a heap of stones. But we've often been back just to stand on the rubble and remember the good times, which gives us a great deal of satisfaction.

'I can still see the secret places where I played "Indians" and went tracking with the seven boys from next door. This turned out to be excellent training for the Services – no wonder I was to become known as Winston and always called upon to lead! In those early days I could get within ten feet of a roe deer without it knowing I was there, but what barks of alarm they gave when they did get on to me.

'I was mostly self-taught, though my brother Jack helped me in a number of ways. I remember the first night I set the snares which he had given me. Next day there was just a rabbit's head left in one of them – a fox had taken the body and I have never forgiven Reynard since.

'I was twelve years old when the war finished. What celebrations there were! We were all given a mug each and I can still see the flags waving on all the churches. But despite the euphoria I felt somewhat cheated as I had *wanted* to play my part in defending the realm.

'Anyway, when I was fourteen, father was a rabbit catcher, having retired from keepering. He also helped on the farm, laying hedges and so on, and I began to assist him. Then Colonel Ogden died and the shoot was let to his son-in-law Devenish, of the brewery family. Walter Shaw came from Norfolk to be headkeeper and lived next door to us.

'Then the estate was sold to Captain Rodd from Devon. Shaw had a lad to help, but he was lazy and got fired, so I was taken on as kennel boy/underkeeper. Gradually I became responsible for improving the partridge population, using the Euston System; I thought the Knebworth System much better, however, using twelve chipped eggs instead of sixteen. We hand-reared the surplus so that they stood a better chance of survival, as did the reduced broods in the care of their parents.

'Then it was all grey partridges, of course. We regarded the redleg as vermin. But in about 1930 Captain Rodd of Turnworth House bought some eggs of the redleg, known to us as Hungarian partridges in those days. These were mixed up with the picked-up greys and distributed over the shoot, the popular idea of the day being to change the blood, but I thought it was a waste of time.

'Our coops were wide apart – twenty-five yards – so that the birds did not congregate, and this gave each covey its own identity. And if I ever caught a

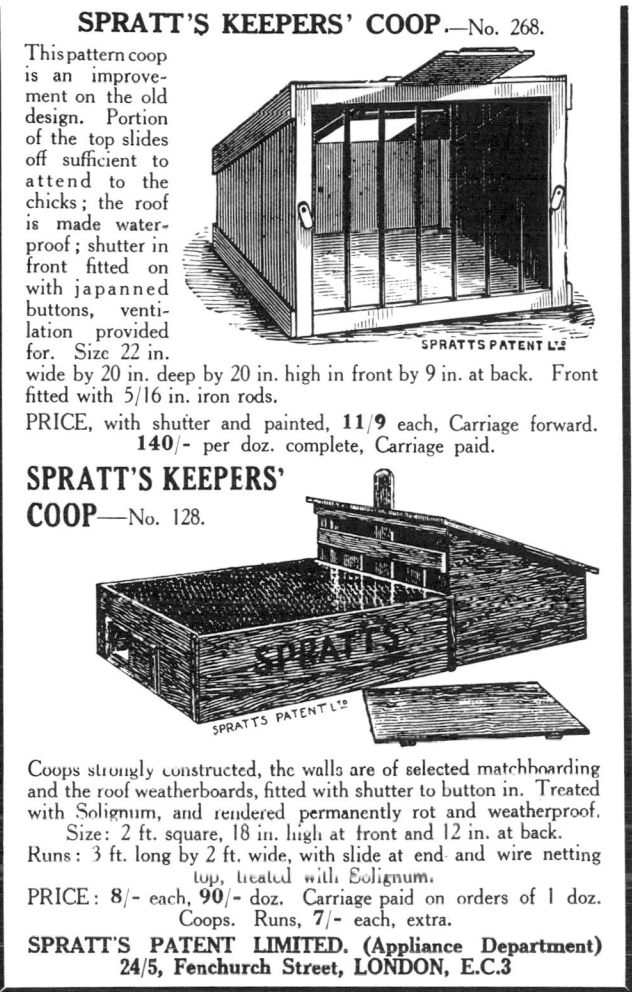

KEEPERS NEED THESE

SPRATT'S KEEPERS' COOP.—No. 268.

This pattern coop is an improvement on the old design. Portion of the top slides off sufficient to attend to the chicks; the roof is made waterproof; shutter in front fitted on with japanned buttons, ventilation provided for. Size 22 in. wide by 20 in. deep by 20 in. high in front by 9 in. at back. Front fitted with 5/16 in. iron rods.

PRICE, with shutter and painted, **11/9** each, Carriage forward. **140/-** per doz. complete, Carriage paid.

SPRATT'S KEEPERS' COOP—No. 128.

Coops strongly constructed, the walls are of selected matchboarding and the roof weatherboards, fitted with shutter to button in. Treated with Solignum, and rendered permanently rot and weatherproof. Size: 2 ft. square, 18 in. high at front and 12 in. at back. Runs: 3 ft. long by 2 ft. wide, with slide at end and wire netting top, treated with Solignum. PRICE: **8/-** each, **90/-** doz. Carriage paid on orders of 1 doz. Coops. Runs, **7/-** each, extra.

SPRATT'S PATENT LIMITED. (Appliance Department) 24/5, Fenchurch Street, LONDON, E.C.3

1932

pheasant on my partridge beat – boot! – up in the air!

'The feed used was millet, hemp, kibbled maize and kibbled wheat. We fed 'em little and often – as in the wild. But ours was good country and they were getting a lot of natural food, too, especially ants' eggs on old meadow land. We used to spade out the sides of the ants' nests and the birds loved it. The ants bring up their larvae to the heat of the sun, you know.

'In those days on my beat we usually shot a hundred brace first day over, the best being 111½ brace, eighty on the second day and fifty to sixty on the third. The rest were left as breeding stock and we moved on to other beats, mine being the best.

'The Hambros' Milton Abbas estate adjoined Turnworth and their partridge beatkeeper Harry Ricketts taught me a great deal. Being neighbours, the Hambros used to come to shoot with us quite a lot. I remember one early occasion when the boss was keen to impress them and instead of placing the Guns on platforms halfway up the chalk hill, we stood them right in the bottom of the valley, known as the Horseshoe. Unfortunately this made the birds far too high for most men and they hit nothing.

'But we always had great fun at Turnworth and everyone really relaxed over lunch. Us keepers and beaters often took ours in the old sawmill. Here there was a simple hole in the ground faced with bricks: one man would stand in the bottom with one above, at each end of a huge handsaw, working along a trunk guided by a chalkline. We often sat with our legs dangling in the sawpit while we ate our rabbit stew (which always included the eyes). One day a Borstal boy came beating and sat there with me. I asked him what he was in for and, ironically, as we peered into the rabbit stew (eyes and all) he replied: "Taking a blind man's dinner when he wasn't looking". But he enjoyed it, just as he did the bottle of mild ale which everyone was given.'

Eventually headkeeper Shaw's son left school and Captain Rodd told Harry he would have to make way for the lad, though he could stay on indefinitely until he found another job. Therefore Harry applied for three of the many jobs advertised in *The Gamekeeper* magazine. The first reply came from Wiltshire, but when Harry told them the terms required he was advised that he was "too experienced for the job": in other words, they did not want to pay too much money. Then he was accepted for a job in Northamptonshire simply on the strength of his letter and references.

SPRATT'S SITUATION REGISTER

Exists for the convenience of gentlemen requiring Gamekeepers and keepers requiring situations. There are no fees. Particulars of situations vacant and Employment required can be furnished by post, or the Register inspected at

24-25, FENCHURCH STREET, LONDON, E.C.3
Gentlemen can also meet Keepers at this address by appointment.

1928

'I didn't even have to go for an interview. They wanted me to start on the Saturday, but I told them I wanted to play my last game of football in Dorset so I would start on the Monday. And just after that I was also accepted for the third job, in Devon.'

Thus in 1934 Harry entered the employment of stockbroker Dennis Capron of Southwick Hall, Northamptonshire. After one year Capron took on two more keepers and more land and Harry was put in charge. He proudly recalls that in 1939: 'For the three beats I had nearly 4,000 English partridge eggs through my hands, and I did all the chipping off myself, with rows of incubators and broody hens.'

Back in Dorset the Guns had always been 'the local gentry – all friends of the boss who took it in turn to shoot with each other, and the word syndicate had never been heard of. But in Northamptonshire there was a gradual change and we started to get a fair sprinkling of self-made men.

'Capron was always interested in the tips we received and used to ask me what I had been given. One day I told him the total was £5 10s for the six guests. "Who gave you the ten shillings?", he demanded. "He'll never shoot here again." And he gave me the ten bob to make up the difference. Mind you, £1 was a good tip then.

'Capron was a real friend to me. I went with him to shoot all over the country, though his valet often did the loading too. One thing I made a point of remembering was where we would get good lunches, and if Capron proposed going somewhere where I knew the food to be poor I used to say "I'm afraid I'll have to stay home tomorrow and send an underkeeper". Us visiting keepers and loaders generally ate in the servants' halls, but we often had the same food as the Guns.

'Mr Capron had a pair of Purdeys and a pair of Holland and Hollands, and always had me carry a huge amount of his clobber, including a mac, gannochy, an extra bag with five hundred cartridges and so on, while he sauntered along with only a shooting stick, always wearing a trilby hat. And he was a fidgety sort of chap, constantly changing position and puffing away at Egyptian cigarettes, some of which he gave me. But every time he moved from his allotted peg I had to pick up all the gear and follow, so one day I said to him: "Look here, are you ever going to keep still?" To my great surprise, he simply said: "OK, we'll stop here".

'He was a good Shot – not surprising really with all that practice. I had a clicker to record his kills and I remember counting sixty-five to his gun at one stand. Mind you, he was made to look ordinary at Helmsley. There was a top Shot on our left, dealing beautifully with the high pheasants, and no way was he in the same class. Birds were falling so far they split open on the rocks. It was cold too. I remember one Gun drooping pheasants' wings over his hands to keep warm between drives on those cold Yorkshire hills.

Overleaf:

Harry Churchill (tenth from left, standing, with hat in left hand) at Southwick Hall on 23 September 1935, when they shot 111½ brace of partridges on his beat, a record for the district. The Guns were: Dennis Capron (sitting centre with spectacles and hat in hand), Charles Chichester (the cousin of Sir Francis Chichester, sitting front, third from right), Charles Heathcote, Roderick Capron and Capt Phillips. Also pictured are the other keepers – Southwick keepers – Len Casey, Jim Wilson and Bob Nunn, the pickers-up and beaters. The game cart is at the back

Harry Churchill clayshooting at one of the annual 'Fox Feasts' put on by the Woodland Pytchley Foxhunt at Southwick in the 1930s

'Generally, I would say that there are not such good Shots nowadays, as the gentry are not brought up to it like they were, especially as they have such freedom of choice and can travel so easily to do whatever they wish. In the old days a youngster was put in the charge of a keeper from the word go, and I am pleased to say I brought many of them along. I always told 'em they could only shoot in front. Today you see most birds shot up the backside by businessmen not brought up to shoot properly.

'Also, the new Gun's lack of knowledge of quarry can be abysmal. I suppose you know the story about Sir Brian Mountain of Eagle Star. Many years ago, on shooting a woodcock, he is said to have exclaimed: "That's a nice little bird – we must rear more!"

'General understanding of other fieldsports used to be better, too – we all tried to help each other and take an interest. For example, at Southwick we used to have an annual Fox Feast, put on by the Woodland Pytchley for all the people whose land they hunted over. All the keepers attended, and there was very keen competition in the clayshoot.'

In 1939 Harry volunteered for the RAF, determined to play his part after 'missing out' on World War I. He wanted to 'get back at Hitler' and subsequently played a valuable role in ground defence.

He was demobbed in 1945 and spent a year or so working for the Ministry of Agriculture on pest control, vermin having proliferated during the war. His main quarry were rats, rabbits and moles, and his best 'bag' was 4,000 rats in one night at Corby refuse dump. 'We had baited the place for two days, and on that third day they were queuing up waiting for the bait.'

With the loss of manpower, there were plenty of jobs to choose from after the war and eventually Harry decided to settle down in 1947 as keeper for Major David Watts-Russell on the Biggin Estate, Benefield, Northamptonshire, where he was to spend the rest of his working life.

His great interest in gundogs and field trials began in 1938, when he bought his first bitch, Teal. Sadly, with the war coming, he had to sell her, and after the war good dogs were hard to come by. But this did not hold him back and he went on to become one of the most celebrated names on the field trial circuit, having the honour of judging *the* Retriever Championship twice, at Ancaster and Cromlix. He has also judged the Irish Championship and the gamekeepers' classes at Crufts on several occasions.

Harry retired from Biggin and full-time keepering in March 1988, at the age of eighty, and even then gave up only because of a troublesome knee – 'It's unfair to continue if you can't do a job 100%.' David Watts-Russell, shortly before he died, also in 1988, said of Harry: 'He has been a natural and instinctive keeper, able and happy to pass on his skills to the younger generation.'

Indeed, Harry remains very active in giving talks to Young Farmers' Clubs, the Women's Institute and other organisations. 'But you have to be selective in what you talk about – nothing too gory for the Girl Guides!' And it was through his ability to present himself enthusiastically and interestingly that Harry came to star in Channel 4's TV special, 'The Shoot', which was very well received.

When I asked Harry if he would do it all again, he replied: 'Oh yes!' Sadly, he has no son to continue the great family tradition, but his daughter is married to a full-time gundog breeder/trainer in Canada, where she has lived and taught since 1964. Harry often visits her there, and was particularly impressed by the gundog trial which was held up for no less than three hours while a huge, migrating flock of Canada geese passed overhead, such was the clamour.

Understandably, he regrets the way commercialism has shaped the profession. 'They're not keepers now: they're just poultry minders. The real art is in knowing all the sounds, signs and tracks of the countryside. In my youth it was almost unheard of for anyone not born into the job to become a keeper.'

Such men of the 'old school' were also fortunate in having the loyalty of wives who expected little in life and were prepared to put up with the hardship and uncertainty. Harry's wife Dorothy was no exception, and after they married in 1935 she took great joy in helping on the rearing field. Later she also helped with shoot teas and welcomed many guest Guns to their humble cottage. In particular, she remembers the Duke of Gloucester coming. 'As he stepped through the door, his

Harry Churchill with one of his old pheasant food choppers

Off to the next stand

The introduction of field glasses made life much easier for the keeper in the apprehension of poachers

A headkeeper, as well as any intelligent assistant, should be provided with a small pair of field-glasses, such as can be bought for a couple of pounds, and taught how to use them. When the glasses are once focussed to suit the man's vision, as used on an object a few hundred yards away, they should be fixed from further movement so as to be instantly available. We recollect a netting case being tried, in which it appeared that two poachers caught after an assault on a keeper in the dark, managed to escape with their booty; but as dawn was breaking the keeper spied them making off in the distance, out of eye-sight, though not beyond the powers of the field-glass he carried. He, though badly wounded, managed to get home, and at once despatched a messenger on horseback to the adjacent town, with a note to the police inspector, giving the names of his assailants. The constables proceeded to the respective homes of the poachers, and took them red-handed; in fact, waited for them to return, which they presently did. The evidence was too strong to be rebutted, and the men pleaded guilty, one remarking to the other as they separated at the dock, 'It's them cussed spectacles (ie field-glasses) as did us, Bill' – a broad hint that was at once acted upon by the local game-preservers to their great advantage, and to the confusion of poachers in that neighbourhood.

As soon as a keeper gets a new situation, it is his duty to make the acquaintance of, and so be able to swear to, all the poaching characters of the locality, but on no account ever to drink with them. Doing so is the first downward step a keeper takes, and a very fatal one.

As to keepers defending themselves against night poachers by carrying guns, it is a mistake to think they do so. A poacher will much sooner shoot a keeper than a keeper a poacher, should both be armed, and so the former gets the first chance of using such a deadly means of defence. It is far better that keepers should carry revolvers, as these weapons are a great deal more effective than guns when a hand-

to-hand struggle for life takes place, and poachers are more afraid of a revolver hidden, or supposed to be hidden, in a keeper's pocket, but yet ready for use, than they are of a gun.

Revolvers, however, require considerable care in their handling, or they are liable to cause accidents to their possessors. The only way to carry a revolver safely in the pocket, so that it cannot be exploded by a fall or a jar, is to take out one cartridge and let the hammer lie on the uncharged chamber. Above all things avoid a cheap revolver, such as is sold by ironmongers for about £1.

However, to fight and risk his life to secure some few pounds' worth of game from poachers is not a keeper's first duty, but to identify and afterwards convict, and for this latter reason a dark lantern, that can be made to instantly flash a man's countenance into his memory, is one of a keeper's most useful weapons. On no account ought a keeper to call a man by name in a poaching affray should he recognise him; many a keeper and watcher have been shot dead by a recognised poacher for doing so, the man determining to commit a murder rather than face certain conviction afterwards. Long and heavy oak sticks have been found more effective for keepers than guns or pistols, and always will be if their owners use them the right way, which is to *thrust* with them at close quarters, and *not* to strike, the latter being usually a wild and useless form of attack.

Health and strength are enjoyed by keepers, probably from the outdoor nature of their avocation, and many an old keeper of seventy is a match for a man, whether friend or poacher, of half his age. A good keeper is rarely on the sick list, or, if ill, is so to an extent that would half kill a weaker man ere he will confess himself unfit for work.

From *Shooting – Field and Covert* by Lord Walsingham and
Sir Ralph Payne-Gallwey, 1885

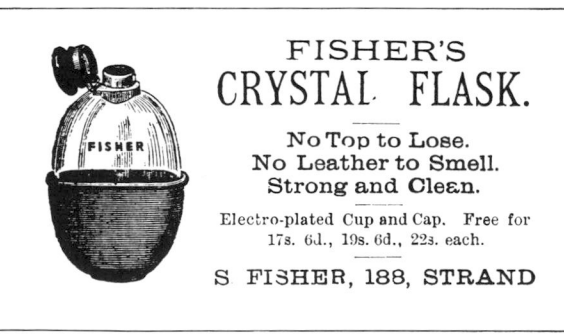

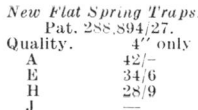
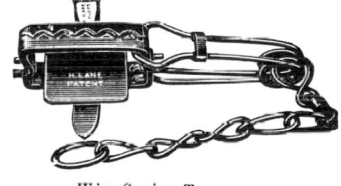

Woodcock Bonus

One day in 1891, headkeeper Marwood of Hawkerland, Devon, took his master's son, E. Pellier Johnson, and another Gun roughshooting through the woods. As they walked along a narrow path in the bracken, a rabbit crossed to the right, which young Pellier Johnson shot as it ascended a bank. While he was taking out the exploded cartridge another rabbit crossed over to the left. Immediately Pellier Johnson closed the gun and took a snap-shot, cutting down a regular lane through the ferns. But they could not see the rabbit and proceeded to look and see if the shot had connected. Imagine their surprise when instead of a rabbit they found two dead woodcock, not together, but at least five yards apart and in the same straight line of fire.

Off the Hook

Postman Joseph Walker of Great Ponton, Lincolnshire was spotted by assistant gamekeeper Fred Moore when he popped a brace of pheasants into his delivery bag in December 1931 – he had removed them from hooks in the game larder at Stoke Rochford, the property of Major R. T. Ellison of Grantham. Fortunately for him, magistrates at Spittlegate Police Court, Grantham took into consideration the defendant's good character and the fact that he had to feed his three children on a part-time postman's wage of 16s 11d per week. He was discharged under the First Offenders' Act.

The Underground Fast

A French gamekeeper living in the Haute Saône had a dog which was much given to foxhunting on its own account. One day in 1894 the dog ran a fox to ground and began a 'set-to' underground. Suddenly, the listening gamekeeper heard something fall, and then there was silence. Either the dog had been killed or the soil had fallen in, so the keeper made an effort to dig the animal out. But as the ground was rocky he failed and, giving up the job, went home, and then forgot him.

One day a neighbour, passing near the spot, heard a faint growl, and at once ran off to tell the gamekeeper, who returned with another friend and some shovels. After just five minutes digging they liberated the poor beast, which was wasted to a skeleton, and whose nose and claws bore witness to the efforts he had made to get out. He had been imprisoned for three weeks, and must have fasted all that time.

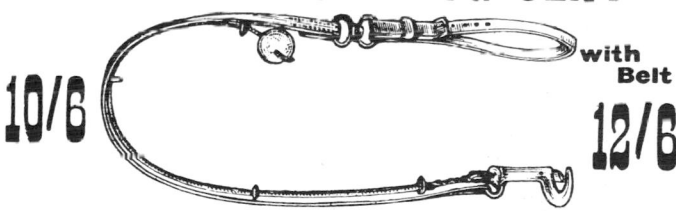
1888

A Cry for Help

A curious accident befell Charles M'Aullay, gamekeeper to Edwin Bolton of West Plean, when he was out on his rounds in February 1895. The double-barrelled gun which he was carrying accidentally slipped off his arm, the butt fell forward and the triggers down, and so the shot went off; the charges partly entered the left foot, creating a bad flesh wound and shattering some of the bones – a number of pellets also struck the dog which accompanied M'Aullay. The accident took place near the Old Glasgow Road, Plean, and M'Aullay cried to a woman passing by for assistance. Medical aid was summoned from Denny, near Falkirk, and was soon in attendance.

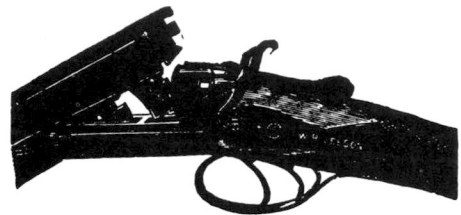
Killed Over a Nest

Andrew Whitley, gamekeeper to Sir Thomas Grove at Pollard Royal, Wiltshire, was indicted for the murder of his uncle, Charles Elford, on 3 August 1884. They had a quarrel about a partridge's nest – the deceased had picked up an iron rod from the sheepfold, but the prisoner had wrested it from him and struck him on the head, fracturing his skull. He was found guilty of manslaughter and Mr Baron Huddleston sentenced him to fifteen years penal servitude.

The Golfer and the Partridge

West Mersea gamekeeper W. Bobby related a strange tale at Lexten and Winstree Sessions in 1932, when Maurice George Johnson of Haycock's Farm was summoned for taking twelve partridge eggs from a nest on land where he was not licensed to kill game. Johnson had been seen by several youths with the eggs in his possession and, presumably realising that this would come to the knowledge of the keeper, he went to the latter and informed him that 'the boy Farthing had taken eleven eggs from a nest on the golf-links'.

Later, Bobby interviewed Farthing and then Johnson, who told a story of how, while on the golf-links, a man playing there had lost a ball and asked him (Johnson) to search for it. While doing this they had found, under a tuft of grass, a hen partridge sitting on a nest. According to the defendant the man had killed the bird with his club, put it in his pocket, and told him to pick up the feathers and take the eggs home.

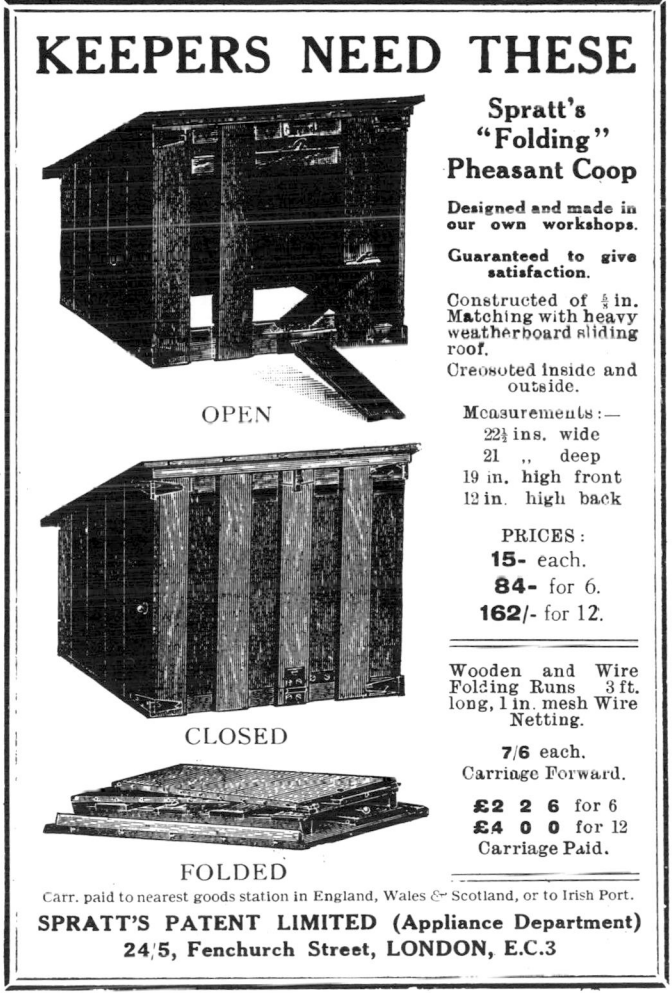
1932

Police followed up Johnson's description of the golfer but soon concluded that no such man existed, and when they challenged the lad he admitted that the story was a 'fake'. He had taken the eggs home for his mother to cook, but apparently she had refused to accept them and had subsequently thrown them away. On another occasion he had said that he wanted them for his collection. Anyway, he was found guilty and bound over for twelve months.

The Keeper's Defences

By the late 1930s poaching was, according to *Shooting Times*, 'hardly as serious as it used to be'. But their correspondent 'Hoverer' remembered the time when on some estates

> the keepers prepared for the poaching season just as thoroughly as for the shooting. Everything was got in readiness to receive the gangs which were certain to come some night or other. Useful ash staves were cut, dried and fashioned, wicker shields to intercept stones were made, stuffing fastened inside the crowns of bowler hats, and coats padded on shoulders and arms where blows were likely to fall. All the keepers had lessons in boxing and ju-jitsu, and this had the result of giving them confidence. Shoes were spiked that no slip might occur when running or wrestling. I remember one piece of advice I heard given: 'If you suspect a gang of having been drinking, do not attack at once; wait till their pot-valour has vanished, which it soon will, and then come to grips.'

'Narvous Injury'

Victorian keeper John Cleever wrote of a poacher who had a claim against a railway company for £400 damages against injury sustained in a smash. When the company's lawyers enquired: 'What sort of injury did you sustain?', the aggrieved replied: 'Narvous injury, sir.'

'To what extent?', asked the lawyer. 'To sich an extent that my old shotgun now wobbles about so much that no longer ago then yesterday I shot at a rabbit and knocked over the best dog in all England. I've raised my claim now to £700, and I'm going to push it until somebody hollers for mercy.'

Eye Knocked Out

Gamekeeper Taylor had his eye knocked out by a stone when he and other watchers came upon six or seven men at midnight, on the estate of the Rev N. Bond of Creech Grange, near Wareham on 19 December 1884. Subsequently, the 'powerful-looking' young man Eli Mullett was committed for trial, charged with being concerned in a serious poaching affray. Several other watchers were also seriously injured by stones and bludgeons, but apart from Mullett all the assailants made good their escape.

CAUGHT IN THE ACT!

TERROR! SURPRISE!! AND CONSTERNATION!!!

Caused to Poachers, Burglars, and other trespassers, by using the New Appliance.

POACHING, BURGLARY, ETC., **IMPOSSIBLE WHERE THIS APPLIANCE IS USED.**

Instantaneous in action. Simple, safe and certain. By disturbing a wire a loud report and instantaneous illumination of the surrounding scenery is caused.

No use poachers "setting" after discharging the appliance, as it frightens all ground game within a mile radius.

This appliance should be used by everyone who has property to protect. It has been pronounced by the experts and head-gamekeepers, who have seen it, to be the best invention ever introduced for the purpose, and one that supplies a long-felt want.

Send for circulars and full particulars, post free, to :

G. PINDER, Firework Manufacturer, EDWINSTOWE, near NEWARK.

Border Raid

Watchers had no recourse to the law when a case recalling the days of Border raiding came before Northumberland magistrates at Hexham in March 1887. The prosecution stated that twenty-six Border men, with black masks over their faces and sheets over their clothes, were seen poaching salmon in the river Rede. A force of police endeavoured to get at them, but were kept back by volleys of stones. The poachers quickly got over the Scottish border, and had a terrible fight there for twenty minutes with the police and the watchers, injuring all their assailants, more or less.

It transpired that the Bench has no jurisdiction, the assaults having been committed in Scotland and the poaching in the Bellingham division.

Shooting in His Sleep

In January 1924 a gamekeeper fell asleep in a pigeon hide with his fingers on the triggers of his gun, and when he woke up some hours later he found that he had discharged both barrels during his slumber. Incredible as this seems, apparently it is not that unusual for people to sleep soundly and remain undisturbed by startling noises around them with which they are very familiar.

LESLIE BUCKLE
Sussex and Kent

Unlike most of the other men in this book, Leslie Buckle did not come from a keepering family, but his father's farming occupation was certainly instrumental in determining his future.

Leslie was born on 4 October 1921 at his father's Mead End Farm, Sway, in the New Forest, then still a very unspoilt and remote corner of Hampshire quite unlike the tourist trap of today. It was a place frequented by gypsies, who often came around to play their wind-up wooden organs in the road. And on the rare occasions when the family had a few spare coppers young Leslie would be sent out with a penny or tuppence for the music-makers.

One day a gypsy woman came to the Buckle door selling reels of cotton, bootlaces and wooden pegs with pieces of cocoa tin round the ends. On her back was a grubby infant wrapped in a blanket, and her eyes lit up when she saw five-year-old Leslie walking most uncomfortably behind his mother. Casually, she asked what the trouble was.

Leslie told me: 'I had a boil on my bum: it had been there for a couple of weeks and was so painful I needed at least three cushions before I could sit down. Going to the loo was a real problem.

'Anyway, the tinker said I should be given the liquor from boiled dock root. So that's what we did – and 'orrible brown stuff it was too. To our amazement the boil came right up and burst within twelve hours and I soon made a full recovery.'

It was in those New Forest days that Leslie first came into contact with a shotgun, though it was not used for sporting purposes. His father was the local horse slaughterer, but he would only undertake this unpopular task if allowed to use his 12-bore!

Leslie also helped his father take the horse hides to Sway railway station, but this was a pleasant task because he was always rewarded with a penny, which he put into the Nestlé's machine to buy 'one very thin slice of chocolate'.

A few years later the family moved to Sussex, Leslie's father becoming the tenant of Huxwood Farm on the Idsworth Estate, near Rowland's Castle, on the Hampshire–Sussex border. Their cottage was right in the middle of a keeper's beat and not surprisingly it was not long before ten-year-old Leslie was helping the beatkeeper with simple chores such as setting traps and feeding pheasants. Indeed, the experience made such an impression on the lad he decided there and then that he wanted to be a gamekeeper.

Sometimes he went beating on a Saturday to earn 3s 6d, and if he was lucky enough to carry a spare cartridge bag for one of the Guns a shiny, silver half-crown

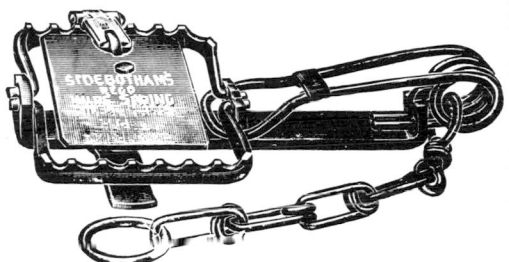
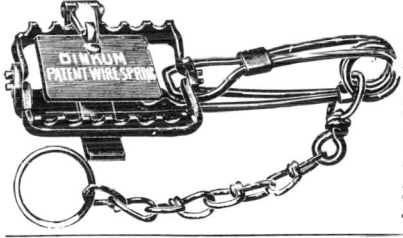

would probably come his way too. At the time all the beaters had to take their own sandwich lunch, but the men were given beer by the estate.

Knowing what he wanted to do in life, Leslie lost interest in school long before the leaving age of fourteen and matters came to a head anyway in the summer, when he was still thirteen. When he announced that he was to play Prince Charming in the school panto his father decided enough was enough. There would be no more 'time wasting' and young Leslie could leave immediately.

At first the lad had to help his father on the farm, and in those days everything was horse-drawn. 'On the farm itself we had a mixture of all sorts – cattle, pigs and so on, but not a lot of anything, including money!'

When he was fifteen, Leslie went to work as a keeper's help for Countess Howe who owned the Idsworth estate, where he had first been so attracted to the keeper's life. And it was close enough for him to travel home to his parents' house each day.

Most unusually, the Idsworth keepers were not allowed to keep dogs: that was a job for estate specialists, as with Lady Howe the shooting took second place to her great passion for field trialling. The estate kennel contained about sixty labradors, pointers and setters, and there was a full-time gundog trainer, Mr Gaunt, as well as two kennelmen and a girl assistant.

'In those days it was only the upper set that went to field trials', said Leslie, 'though there were keepers' trials.' These were always two-day events at Idsworth and Lady Howe always bought the winning dog. Apparently keepers could only enter if they agreed to let Lady Howe buy the winning animal. And although she

1880's

always had black labradors, when a yellow dog won in 1938 she had no hesitation in paying a hundred guineas for it – an enormous sum in those days.

On his first day there, Leslie accompanied the headkeeper to a hut in the woods where they collected a bag of whole maize – no problem for the pheasants to deal with in October. Then they marched around the beat together, feeding birds along the way, and thereafter Leslie was left alone to get on with it. His other duties included setting vermin traps, but whereas the other keepers had new or sound ginns, Leslie had to make do with old ones, putting blocks of wood under the weak mechanism so that they would spring better.

In those days there were many more stoats and weasels to be dealt with as there were so many more rabbits and other prey for them to feed on. But the keepers did not resent these pests too much as selling their skins was just about the only 'legal' way they could supplement their modest income. Grade I stoat skins fetched 1s 6d each. They were tagged and, when there were enough, a batch was sent to Friends, the fur and feather merchants, who also took jays' wings for fly-tying and hat decoration.

Eventually a 12s 6d postal order would arrive, 'but that was only enough to buy one boot', remembered Leslie. 'So then you had to wait ages to gather enough to buy the other. Horse-hide boots were the only really waterproof ones. The hides were tanned in the Black Forest by Krupps and we bought the boots from a firm in Scotland, but as far as I know you can't get the like of 'em now.'

Tips were very modest on an estate where every shoot was a field trial. But Lady Howe did give boy Buckle £5 at the end of each rearing season, as a special thank-you for work well done, before she went off to Scotland for grouse shooting. 'When she gave it to me I really thought I was a millionaire and couldn't get home quick enough on my bike. Apparently she gave me the same as the other keepers and the head always told me to keep quiet about it as I was only a lad and the men might object.

'My old BSA was a damn good bike – Father bought it at Havant market for 16s. The headkeeper had a little van and I can still remember its number plate – COT 643. We always made sure we knew all the local number plates so that we knew when strange vehicles were prowling about. Every other car contained someone out from Portsmouth trying to knock our pheasants off. But there was only one local trouble-maker. He was *the* poacher and was caught every other year, but he didn't mind if it was at the end of the season as he used to say that getting put away for a few months helped the winter along. Earlier on he was more careful as most of his business had still to be done.'

When he was eighteen Leslie became a keeper's help on the Little Green estate, working for Sir Philip Reckitt of 'Reckitt's Blue', and 'Reckitt and Colman Mustard' fame. As it was close by he still lived with his parents, 'but instead of going up the lane, I cycled down it'.

The move brought more money: at Idsworth he had started on 15s a week and ended on 22s 6d, but at Little Green he started on 30s. He had heard of the job on the grapevine and secured it through the influence of his father, who was known to the estate.

In addition, he was given a yearly clothing allowance of £8 10s, which bought

Leslie Buckle, aged nineteen, in his keeper's uniform

the traditional 'salt 'n pepper', three-piece tweed suit, two pairs of long johns, a pair of black leather leggings and a matching cap. That was in the year war broke out.

At Little Green the shooting was on a much grander scale than Leslie had been used to, and eleven keepers were employed to provide eighteen consecutive days of double-gun shooting, Sundays excluded, beginning in late November. The concentration was on pheasants, though there were a few early partridges as well.

During the entire three weeks Leslie had to load for the estate's agent, Mr Orr. 'He never missed a day's shooting and got more out of the estate than both Mr Reckitt and Mr Colman, who came into it later with Tommy Sopwith. Orr was sloshed most of the time, only ever grunted and never tipped me, but then he was a Scot. He even had his own chauffeur, housekeeper, butler and boot-boy as well as all the free shooting anybody could ever want.'

In complete contrast was the headkeeper, a kind man who had so much responsibility yet could not read or write.

The beaters were paid 6s 6d a day, which was rounded up to £2 for a six-day week to encourage them to stay on.

At Little Green there were two hundred pheasant coops to a forty-acre (16ha) field, and the three keepers working a field thought they were doing well to average fourteen six-week-old poults to a coop, having started with twenty chicks. All the birds were reared under broody hens.

Throughout the rearing programme the birds were kept as wild as possible and grew up almost wary of man. 'That's why they flew so much better in our day', says Leslie. 'Not like the pathetic things you have to teach to fly today.'

When the pheasants were given their first feed of the day at 7am, the shutters were removed from each coop and laid alongside so that in the evening they could be picked up quickly to shut the birds in again. In the morning the birds would not even come out of their coops until the keeper had moved away, despite the calling of the hens. And when the time came to shut them in for the night it was essential to creep up and pop the shutter over in a flash, otherwise the chicks would scatter in all directions. But some always managed to slip away on the first circuit of the

1932

field and it was often necessary to go round several times, trying to remember which coops remained to be dealt with. This often went on till 10pm or later, despite the fact that the keepers had to be up to let the birds out again at 7am.

But those were far more labour-intensive days – one of the major chores was moving all the coops every day so that the birds were always on fresh grass. And on each occasion young Leslie also had to swing the scythe right across that forty-acre field.

Even on the day the coops were moved into the woods the routine had to be adhered to. The poults were taken off at dead of night so that they would settle down better in their new surroundings. A sack was slid under each coop and the four corners tied together at the top before it was loaded onto a horse and cart. The entire operation had to be completed by 6am so that the birds had time to settle before the first feed at 7am.

When all the poults were accustomed to the wood, first the hens and then the coops were taken away, one or two at a time, until eventually the pheasants were living entirely wild.

In 1939 Leslie returned to the Idsworth estate as a beatkeeper, but the war put a stop to rearing and in 1941 young Buckle was called up to the Navy, in which he became an ack-ack gunner. He sailed on the *Cairo* to Scotland, Gibraltar and Malta, but on his second Malta convoy they were sunk by a U-boat and had to jump into an escort vessel. The *Eagle* and the *Manchester* went down with them.

Leslie was taken to Gibraltar before coming back home on the *Nelson*, being transferred to Rossyth and then sent on a special train to Portsmouth. 'My parents knew that the *Cairo* had gone down, but none of us had been able to send word that we were alive. And I knew that we would not be able to telephone from Portsmouth, so when the train went through our village I scribbled a message on my lifebelt and threw it out of the window. Luckily it landed on someone's garden path and they contacted my parents to tell them I was all right.'

Life on board *Cairo* had certainly provided variety and adventure, but perhaps the most interesting trip for Leslie was that to Mermansk in Russia in February, 1942. They took back a party of Russians who had been studying production in British factories, and they returned with a cargo of gold bullion – payment to the USA for arms supplied.

There was further action, too, on a minesweeper and then on the *Belfast* on D-Day.

When he was home on leave in 1942 Leslie married one of his childhood sweethearts from Idsworth. 'During my courting days I used to call in regularly for a cup of cocoa at 9.45pm after my keepering rounds, and I always gave her mum a rabbit and a couple of swedes. With the occasional game of darts in the evening that was the limit of my social life in those days.

'Apparently I always stank of skinned stoat when I went a courtin', but of course I did not notice it like they did. And years later when I was at another estate and happened to skin a stoat my wife said "God, what's that smell?" "Oh, isn't it horrible," I replied. "No, no, I like it", and she added – "It reminds me of you years ago when we were courting."'

After the war Leslie was unable to return to his old job as it had already been

1932

taken by somebody else. So he took a position as a single-handed keeper at Uppark, near Harting, Sussex, for Admiral Meade Fetherstonehaugh – and once again it was his father's farming connection which had paved the way. As a married man, Leslie was greatly attracted by the rent-free cottage which went with the job.

There was very little rearing in those days and all Leslie had to do was look after a few wild pheasants and control the rabbits. In fact, although he had a very fine pair of Boss 12-bores, the Admiral did not even shoot. So the only rearing Leslie did at Uppark was of a hundred or so turkeys for the Christmas market, but even though it was his idea the profits went to the Admiral. Mind you, he did have a bird or two for himself.

At the time, food was still rationed so the turkeys had to live wild and fatten on beechnuts. But Leslie also gave them clayder (goose grass), eggs, onions and chopped stinging nettles 'for the iron'. Each evening the birds went to roost in the beech trees. And this peaceful regime of turkey rearing combined with roughshoot keeping continued for eleven years.

Then came four years as headkeeper for gamefeed manufacturers F. C. Lowe & Sons (run by the Voucher brothers) at Otterden in Kent. The shoot was leased from the Wheeler family and Leslie had two underkeepers plus his eldest daughter to help him continue with the open-field rearing system, at a time when most other estates had changed to the Cotswold System. Lowe's made feed for open rearing so this was not surprising: 'we were probably the last estate in the country still using the system'.

In 1960 Leslie was invited to become headkeeper for Frederick Edward Neuflize Ponsonby, the tenth Earl Bessborough at Stansted Park, Sussex, and Leslie was pleased to accept as it meant both he and his wife could return to their native haunts. And he is there to this day.

At first there were four underkeepers and they put down 7 or 8,000 birds a season. Today Leslie, in so-called retirement, works with only one pensioner and two lads, yet still puts down some 5,000 birds. He regrets the trend which had made keepers more like poultry farmers, but there is no way that so many birds could be reared by so few men today using the old methods with broody hens.

Poaching has always been a considerable problem at Stansted as more and more people own cars and swarm out from neighbouring towns such as Portsmouth. But Leslie has always enjoyed great support from local police and there have been only two occasions when he was in some danger.

'The first happened on a Sunday morning, when a father and his two sons knocked me into a ditch. I had blocked the road with my Land Rover and one of them came at me with a spider wheel-brace. I was knocked out for a while and when I came to one of the men was still over me thumping me for all he was worth. But I managed to get my thumb inside his mouth and heave him off.

'I was just beginning to get the better of my attacker when the other keeper came back from phoning the police. He came up on the father who was watching his son grapple with me and smashed him on the head with the butt of a .22 rifle. The old poacher had a big, grey overcoat on and I'll never forget the sight of him as he crumpled unconscious into the hedge, the huge, bloody collar coming right up around his face. I thought we'd killed him. And on top of that my keeper colleague seemed to go berserk, swinging at everything and everybody within reach, smashing the windscreen of the poachers' van.

'Meanwhile, the other son had driven my Land Rover off down the lane and crashed into a fence-post, so we had to go and retrieve it to get the old boy to hospital. But when we came back we found that the other son had somehow managed to get his father into their Mini van and driven off with him.

'We gave chase down the track and the little van soon got stuck in some water, but while we were so intent the poacher who had been put in the back of the Land Rover jumped out and ran off.

'Then we drove in front of the van, but as we did so they managed to start the engine and reversed down the lane, only to find the police waiting for them. I can tell you it gave me great pleasure to see them all handcuffed – though at the same time they handcuffed the keeper who had assaulted the poacher with his gun.

'The trial lasted two days at Chichester Crown Court and the poacher who attacked me was given four months suspended for two years. Later they came up for the poaching offence at the magistrates' court, where they were all fined and had their guns confiscated. The police decided not to prosecute the other keeper for his assault.

'On another occasion, at about 5pm I heard air-rifle shots coming from the pheasant pen just opposite my house. And when I crept over I saw a man and a woman killing the birds. He was the marksman and she the picker-up with a canvas holdall.

'When they saw me they made a run for it. There was no way I could catch the fellow as he was much younger than me and had light shoes on whereas I was lumbered with wellies. But I caught the woman and then the fellow came back. He aimed his gun at me, but I told him not to be so stupid and as I walked towards him he fled again.

'I asked her what was in the bag. She said I was not going to see and hurled it into the bushes over the fence. Then I walked down the road with her so that I could at least see their vehicle and get the number.

'We were only about twenty yards along the main road when the fellow came back, and as I turned he hit me and knocked me down, but I was still conscious. Then the girl put the boot in and called out "Give it to him, John!"

'My main thought was to get the gun away from him and we fell struggling onto the bank. I managed to grab the gun and held it away from him with one arm while I held him back with the other. With a great effort I was just able to toss the gun up and away, but it hit the top strand of the barbed wire fence and bounced back into the road. And all the time I was shouting for help.

'Then the girl picked up the gun, but luckily enough a car came along and stopped, and my wife appeared from the house. She immediately telephoned the police.

'Then came another car with a petty officer in and he turned out to be quite useful, pinning the man against the fence until the law arrived. Very soon there were police all over the place – cars and motor bikes in all directions. They were marvellous, the local boys from Westbourne.'

As a result of the attack, Leslie had to go into hospital for two days so that a surgeon could ease out the dent in the side of his skull and relieve pressure on nerves. This injury surprised them all as he had not been rendered unconscious. In recent years, however, the injury has been troublesome.

The airgunner was given a suspended sentence and fined. The woman had to pay damages to Leslie – 'Every month I had a cheque for a pound or two in the post. She had been in all sorts of trouble and was a real gangster's moll. I also received £750 from the Criminal Injuries Board.'

Despite these setbacks and a not unexpected degree of gun deafness, life at Stansted has been very satisfying for Leslie and he has enjoyed serving the Earl, born 1913. 'Lord Bessborough is a good and keen Shot but, like me, he is understandably slowing up a bit now.

Leslie Buckle outside his keeper's lodge at Stansted Park in 1988

'We still manage some fifteen days shooting and enjoy a constant stream of interesting guests. We have had King Constantine, and one of my favourites has been Lord Hailsham, who generally comes every year, usually on Boxing Day, and stays for a couple of days. He's a real gentleman and always writes to thank me as soon as he gets home. We really get on well together and I think that if ever I told him I was a bit pushed he'd find a job for me in the House of Lords!'

Today Leslie continues to judge gundog tests, but not trials as he is too busy in the winter, though he does trial a dog sometimes. And he is extremely well organised by his second wife, who works in the estate office and does much of the shoot's paperwork.

As far as he knows, Leslie is not related to the famous nineteenth-century Buckle keepers of Merton, Norfolk, but he does have a younger brother in keepering at Alton, Hampshire. He does not have a son to follow in his footsteps but his three-year-old grandson has already learnt to set snares and loves playing with grandad's ferret. He will have a lot to live up to.

INDEX

Page numbers in *italics* indicate illustrations

ACCIDENTS, 39, 55, 56, 58–9, 60, 72, 73, 100, 118, 144, 170
Ack-ack, 37, 126, 179
Acton Burnell, Shropshire, 27
Adisham, Kent, 55
Aeroplanes, 72–3
Afghans, 43, 93
Airguns, 182
Alarms, *76*, 138
Ale, 143
Algiers, 87
Alton, Hampshire, 125–9, 184
America, 109, 179
Ammerdown Park, Somerset, 118
Ancaster, Lincs, 156
Arkengarthdale, Yorks, 87
Armistice, the, 121
Army, the 41, 43, 44, 45, 47
Ascot, Berkshire, 19
Ashburton, Lord, 25
Asquith family, 121–2
Astley, John, 144
Atholl, Duke of, 39
'Auld Lang Syne', 69
Australia, 60

BADGERS, 4, *12*, 130
Badsworth Hall, 48
Bags, 10, 20, 34, 40, 43, 44, 69, 70, 78, 80, 84, 85, 93, 94
Bailey, Lady Janet, 70
Baker, Fred T., gunmaker, 165
Ballinasloe, 55
Barclay, Capt C. G. E., 17
Barclay, Col H., 134
Barclay, Maj M. E., 17
Basking shark, 53
Bath, Lord, 118, 121
BBC, 30, 37, 39
Beaters, 17, 27, 30, 34, 44, 45, 68, *68*, 76, 85, 92, 93, 95, *105*, 120, 172, 178
Bedfordshire, 134
Beer, 27, 28, 34, 69, 76, 85, 114, 143, *143*
Bees, 124
Bell, Henry, 66, 72
Bellows, 80
Belvoir Estate, Notts, 135
Benefield, Upper, Northants, 159
Bermuda, 129
Berthon, Col C. P., 60
Bessborough, Earl of, 181, 182
Bicycles, 15, *137*, 175
Biggin Estate, Northants, 156–9
Binoculars, 161
Bird scaring, 74
Birds of prey, 92
Blackerite, 159
Bland, headkeeper, 45
Blenheim, Oxon, 125–9
Boar shooting, 87

Bobby, W., 167
Bolton, Edwin, 166
Bond, Rev N., 169
Bonset, Joseph, 144
Boots and shoes, *71*, *147*, 175
Borders, 169
Borstal boy, 150
Boss guns, 180
Boulton and Paul, 174
Bowood, Wilts, 87
Boxing, 72
Boxing Day, 20, 37, 126, 184
Brabourne, Lord, 23, 47, 70
Brackley, Lord and Lady, 25
Bracknell, 19
Brandon Ferrie, 65
Brandon Station, 85
Breadmaking, 148
Bricklayers, 83
'Brideshead', 30
Bristol, 118, 120
Broadlands, Hants, 23, 65, 70, 71, 72, 138
Brockhurst, Fort, 15
Brockwood, Hants, 87
Broody hens, 10, 29, 31–3, 35, 90, *108*, 178
Broughton, Clwyd, 56
Brown, Ian, 71
Brymer, Wilfred, 74, 76, 77
BSA motor cycles, 114
Buckby, Charles, 144
Buckingham, Cecil, 4, *12*–15
Buckinghamshire, 134
Buckle, Israel, 80
Buckle, Leslie, 172–84, *176*, *183*
Bulbarrow, Dorset, 148
Bulls, 85–6
Burmese, 93
Bury St Edmunds, 72
Butlers, 116, 118, 122, 177
Buxton, Lord, 38

CAGEBIRDS, 129
Cairo, HMS, 179
Cambridgeshire, 17–25
Camphor, 92
Canada, 157
Candles, 52
Capron, Dennis, 151, *152*–3
Capron, Roderick, *152*–3
Carnarvon, Lord, 126
Carpenters, 75, 83
Cars, 85
Cartland, Barbara, 25
Cartridge extractor, *121*
Cartridge reloading, 77
Cartridges, *109*
Carts, 33, 66, 76, 92, 147, 148, 179
Casey, Len, *152*–3
Castle Howard, 30 40
Catching-up, 35, 80

Cats, 27, 92, *104*
Cecil, Lord Eustace, 147
Ceylon, 35
Chamberlain, Alice, 147
Chandler, John, 69
Chapmanslade, Wilts, 54
Charles, HRH Prince, 47, 70, 71, 87, *127*, 129
Chatsworth, 47
Chauffeurs, 116
Chawton, Hants, 125–9
Chesham, Lady, 89
Chesham, Lord, 83, 87, 89
Cheshire, 114
Chester-le-Street, Durham, 65
Chichester, Charles, *152*–3
Chiddingfold, Surrey, 94
Children, 120, 125
Christian, Claude, 133
Christmas, 37, 40, 68–9, 93, 95, 117, 125, 180
Churchill, Harry, 148–59, *152*, 154–5, *157*
Churchill, Odette, 43
Churchill, Winston, 43, 126
Cider, 143, *143*
Clark, Jack, 41–7, *42*, *46*
Clark, Nobby, 41, *42*
Claypigeon shooting, 154–5, 156
Cleever, John, 167
Clement, Lewis, 57, 98
Climbing keepers, 105
Cobham, Kent, 60
Cobley, Thomas, 144
Cocoa, 76
Cohen, Eliot, 125
Coke of Norfolk, 59
Collingham, Notts, 113
Colpit, Bob, 66
Combe, Richard, 20
Comet shops, 40
Condover, Shropshire, 27
Conisborough, Yorks, 133
Constantine, King, 184
Coopic, 83
Coops, 75, 83, 90–1, 92, 126, 148, *149*, 166
Coot, headkeeper, 21
Coot shooting, 20
Copley, Edward, 48
Copse shooting, 102
Corbett, V. C. S. W., 110
Corby, Northants, 156
Cotswold System, 181
Cottages, keepers', *13*, *139*, *159*
Country Life magazine, 122
Coursing, 66
Cousins, A. A., 108
Crack Shots, 110, 126
Crafts, 66
Creosote, 35, 41
Criminal Injuries Board, 182

Cromlix, 156
Crow, carrion, 35, 54, *54*
Crufts, *14*, 17, 20, 114, 156
Cudworth, Yorks, 50
Cumbrian wrestling, 69
Cunningham-Reid, Capt R. F. C., 21
Cunningham-Reid, Noel, 25
Curtis, Squire, 113

DADLEY, E. R., 17, 25
Dalham Hall, 69
Dancing and singing, 69
Darnley, Earl, 60
Darwin, Charles, 94
Darwin, Philip, 94
Davenport, Maurice E., 98
Dawling, headkeeper, 113
Deacon, Col, 34, 37
Death duties, 122
Deer, 20, 140, *140*, 148, 192
Denaby, Yorks, 133
Denbigh, Clwyd, 57
Deopham, Norfolk, 125
Derbyshire Yeomanry, 69
Devenish brewery, 148
Devon, 164
Dialects, 66
Dickinson of Rowntrees, 37
Disease, 92
Disney, Albert, 100, 135
Dogs, 33, 37, 165
Dog lead, *165*
Dominoes, 61
Donkeys, 113, 114, 148
Dorchester, 76
Dorset, 75–82; 146–50, *151*, 169
Douglas-Home, The Hon William, 25
Drinking fountains, 180
Drugs, 42
Duck shooting, 20, 41, 114
Duckworth, Major, 121
Duckworth-Chad, Anthony, 47
Dudmaston Hall, Shropshire, 27, 28
Dunley, Hants, 78
Durham, 65–6
Durham, Earl of, 65
Durno, Joe, 31, *32*, 37

EAGLE, GOLDEN, 143
Eagle, HMS, 179
Eagle Star Insurance Co, 78, 156
Eaton, Cheshire, 65
Edinburgh, Duke of, 47
Edward VIII, King, 19, 44
Edward, Prince, 47
Eggs, artificial, 55, 159
Egyptian cigarettes, 151
Elford, Charles, 166
Elizabeth II, Queen, 47, 138
Ellisfield, Hants, 134
Elmsthorpe, Leics, 144
Elveden, Suffolk, 65, 73
English gamekeepers, 109
Euston, Suffolk, 65
Euston System, 148
Evans, Sgt, Denbigh, 57
Everitt traps, *113*

FAKES, STELLA, 89
Fakes, Wally, 83–9, *84*, 88
Falcon, peregrine, 81
Farming, 69, 85, 87, 90, 93, 114, 172, 174, 180
Feeding game, 12, 33, 34, 41, 66, 74, 84, 85, 90, 91, 92, 99, *103*, 114, *115*, *119*, 146–7, 149, 175, 178, *178*, 186
Fellowes, Lady, 43
Fellowes, Sir William, 43

Fenston, Felix, 122, 124
Ferrets and ferreting, 35, *101*, 114, 131, 141, *141*, 184
Feversham, Lord, 30
Field, Mr Justice, 59
Field magazine, 29
Field glasses, 161, *161*
Field trials, 156, 174
Filton, Bristol, 37
Fines, 50
Finns, 78
Firewood, 42
Fish, 53
Fisher's crystal flask, 162
Flask, drinking, *162*
Fletcher, Hamilton, 134
Fletcher, Patrick, 54, 136
Flitcham, Norfolk, 41
Flowers, *10*, 114–15
Fluke shots, 164
Food boilers, *34*
Food chopper, *157*, 159
Football, 151
Forbes, Major, 114
Ford, Henry, 70
Forte, Lord, 124
Fox, headkeeper, *35*
Foxes, 21, 27, 28, 31, 33, 34, 52, *52*, 58–9, *58*, 82, 86, 92, 131, *132*, 142, *142*, 143–4
Foxhunting, 59–9, 81, 146, 147, 165
France and the French, 87, 102, 165
Frensham, Surrey, 20–1
Friends, fur and feather merchants, 175
Frome, River, 78, 81
Froome, J., 134
Funerals, *42*, 121, 126

GALWAY GAOL, 55
'Galloping Major' (song), 68
Gallimore, poacher, 57
Gamebags, *120*
Gamebooks, 25, 44
Game carts, 95, 97, 114, *152–3*
Game Conservancy, 122
Gamekeeper and Countryside Magazine, 12, 77, 114, 118, 150
Gamekeepers' Association, 125
Game larder, 20, 164
Game prices, 97
Gamekeeper, the ideal, 47
Gapes, 33, 80, 92, 159
Gardening, 40, 114, 116
Geeson, Joseph, 135
Gentian, 92
George V, King, 45, 47
George VI, King, 40
Germans and Germany, 102, 116
Gibbs, gunmakers, 118
Gibraltar, 179
Gill, Bill, 90–5, *91*
Gill, Gladys, 94
Gillamoor, Yorks, 30
Ginger beer, 85
Ginn traps, 21, 27, 30, 35, 74, 85, 92, 113, *162*, *173*, 175
Girl Guides, 156
Gittus, Mr, 69
Gladstone, Prime Minister, 56
Glensaug, the, 143
Gloucester, Duke of, 157–8
Godalming, Surrey, 90
Golf, 129, 167
Gosling, Sir Donald, 94, 95
Gosport, Hants, 15
Grafham School, Surrey, 90
Grafton, Duke of, 37
Grantham, Lincs, 100, 164

Grass, Harry, 23, 65–73, *73*
Great Ponton, Lincs, 164
Great Shoots, The, 190
Great Wilbraham, Cambs, 41
Great Yarmouth, 113
Greaves, 53
Green, Edward, 55
Grimthorpe, Lord, 31, 34, 37
Grit, 34
Ground Game Act, 138
Grouse shooting, 87, 131–2, 175
Grove, Sir Thomas, 166
Grundy, keeper, 60
Gypsies, 57, 72, 172
Gunpowder, 113
Gundogs, 47, 53, 65, 81, 98, *98*, *128*, 156, 157, 168, 174, 184
Guests, 78

HAILSHAM, LORD, 184
Hall Barn, 19
Hambro family, 149
Hamilton, Lord, 94
Hampshire, 15, 60, 75–82, 83–9, 125–9, 134, 138
Hardwick, Shropshire, 28
Hardy, Thomas, 146
Hares, 39, 59, *59*, 66, *112*, *144*
Harley-Davidson motorbike, 117
Harrison, Dr Chester, 56
Harrison, M., 110
Havant, Hants, 175
Hawarden, Clwyd, 56
Hawks, 100, 130
'Hawk' bird killer, *125*
Hawkerland, Devon, 164
Hawkins, Jim, 65
Hazeborough Lighthouse, 114
Headkeeper, the, 64, 84
Heathcote, Charles, *152–3*
Hedgehogs, 50, *50*
Helmingham Hall, Suffolk, 47
Helmsley, Yorks, 25, 151
Henniker, Lord, 66, 69, 72
Herbert, Sandford, 144
Hermitage, the, 65, 72
Hertfordshire, 143
Hexham, 169
Hicks, Squire, 41
Hilborough, Norfolk, 83
Hilton Park, 50
Hitler, 74, 156
Holidays, 78
Holkham, Norfolk, 59, 65
Holland and Holland guns, 151
Hollingbury, Mr, 40
Hollington, Berks, 125
Holt, Col, 30
Home Guard, 72, 99
Hoops, 85
Hooton Roberts, Yorks, 133
Hope, Shropshire, 56
Hop-pickers, 122
Hopscotch, 85
Horses, 19, 60, 66, 76, 85, 92, 95, 114, 121, 147, 172, 179
Horsley, Thomas, 76
Hotels, 54
Hounds, 146, 147
'Hoverer', 58, 61, 62–3, *101*, 109, 139, 168
Howard, Lady Cecilia, 37, 39
Howard, The Hon Simon, 40
Howard, Lord George, 30, 37, 39–40
Howe, Countess, 174–5
Huddleston, Mr Baron, 166
Hudson, Thomas, equipment, *180*
Humane killer, *125*
Hunt, Frank, 113–24, *119*, *124*

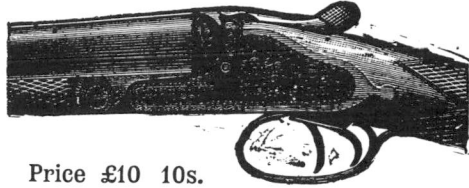
Hurricane lamps, 34
Hurricane planes, 37
Hussey, Mr, 122
Huston, Charles, 94, 122
Hut, keeper's, 33, 61, 61, 91
Hutton, M., 100
Hygiene, 92
Hylton, Lord, 118, 121–2
Hythe, Hants, 60

IDENTIFIERS, 168
Idsworth Estate, Sussex, 172–5, 179
Illingworth, William, 48, 50
Ilsington, Dorset, 74, 78
India, 35, 93
Ingatestone, Essex, 104
Ireland and Irish keepers, 62–3, 108, 156
Isle of Wight, 148
Italy, 44
Italians, 12
Iveagh, Lord, 73

JACK SNIPE, 80
Japanese, 93
Jays, 112
Jelley, Simon, 94
Jeyes Fluid, 41
Johnson brothers, 28
Johnson, E. Pellier, 164
Joliffe, Capt, 118, 121, 122
Jones, Evan, 56
Jones, R. B. H., 48

KAMLIN, 33
Keepering vocation, 101
Keepers' Benefit Society, 96
Keeper's Day, 132
Keepers' defences, 168
Keepers' pleasures, 130–2
Keepers' qualities, 9, 162
Keepers as servants, 9
Keeper's standing, 10
Keith, Sir Kenneth, 25
Kennel boy, 65, 74, 125, 148
Kennels, 174
Kent, 55, 60, 122
Kestrels, 31
Kilminster, 121
Kimberley, Earl of, 113
Kirbymoorside, Yorks, 30
Kirkintilloch, Strathclyde, 144
Knebworth System, 148
Knight, Edward, 129
Knightsbridge, 116
Knives, 72, 121
Knuckleduster, 21, 21
Krupp's boots, 175
Kynaston, Col John, 29
Kynaston, Col Walter, 28

LADY POACHERS, 135, 182
Lake, Wiltshire, 70
Lambton Castle, 65, 66, 72
Lancashire, 125
Lane's traps, 162
Langford Hall, Notts, 113

Latimer, Bucks, 87
Laver, Arnold, 77
Lazslo, Patrick de, 179
Leeson, W. R., guns, 166
Leicestershire, 144
Lemonade, 76
Lennon, P C, 104
Lice, 31
Lights, 52
Limewash, 33, 41, 83
Lincolnshire, 164
Lister, Edward, 137
Little Green Estate, Sussex, 175–9
Livermere, Suffolk, 83
Lloyds Bank, 94
Loading, 25, 73, 87, 99, 118, 126, 136, 177
Lofthouse, Cleveland, 59
Longwood Estate, Hants, 77, 82
London, 71, 76
Longleat, Wilts, 136
Long-service awards (CLA), 40, 47, 87, 127, 129
Looker, Joseph, 104
Lords, House of, 184
Loren, Sophia, 40
Lowe, F. C. & Son, 181
Lowther, John, 59
Lunches, 28, 30, 39, 45, 71, 76, 85, 92, 95, 116, 118, 120, 129, 146, 147, 150
Lurchers, 49, 146
Luton Hoo, Beds, 65
Lyon, Ronnie, 78
Lytchett Matravers, Dorset, 147

MACCLESFIELD, Cheshire, 98
Macey, Len, 74–82, *75, 79, 80*
Macintyre, Dugald, 53
Magpies, 35, 55, 69
Mahon, William, 55
Maidment, Frank, 144
Mallard, 78
Malta, 179
Malton, Yorks, 37
Man, Joseph, 143
Manchester, HMS, 179
Mangel-wurzels, 17
Maps for partridges, *16*, 45
Marbles, 85
Market reports, 97
Market Harborough, 85
Marlborough, Duchess of, 125
Marlborough, Duke of, 125, 126
Marwood, headkeeper, 164
Mayes, Stella, 66
McAlpine, Jimmy, 29
McAlpine, Sir Robert, 122
McAullay, Charles, 166
McCorquodale brothers, 25
McDonald, Jimmy, 41
Meade Fetherstonehaugh, Admiral, 180
Meldrum, Bill, 138
Melton, Notts, 135
Merrett's falcon kite, *162*
Merton, Norfolk, 12, 108, 184
Metcalf, Thomas, 59
Michael of Kent, Prince, 94
Middleton Foxhounds, 31
Milford, Lord, 69, 70
Miller-Munday, Maj, 137
Milne, Alisdair, 39
Milton Abbas, Dorset, 149
Miners, 120
Ministry of Agriculture, 156
Moffatt, keeper, 60
Moles, 124, 156
Monks, Bill, 126
Monte Carlo, 116
Moore, Fred, 164
Morpeth, Viscount, 40
Motor cycles, 29, 98, 114, 117
Mountain, Sir Brian, 78, 156
Mountbatten, Earl, 23, 25, 65, 70, 71
Mountbatten, Countess, 70
Mulgrave, near Whitby, 60
Mullett, Eli, 169
Murder, 50, 55, 59–60, 166
Muzzle-loaders, 113

NATEBY, Lancs, 125
Navy, Royal, 179
Nawton Towers, 30
Nelson, HMS, 179
Nestboxes, 32–3, 35, 83, 90
Nestlé's chocolate, 172
Nets, 57
Newark, Notts, 113
New Forest, 172
Newman, Paul, 40
Newmarket, 17
New Milton, Hants, 125
Nightwatching, 19, 35, 42, 51, *51*, 72, 75, 84, 126, 169
Niven, David, 40
Nore Shoot, Surrey, 94
Norfolk, 15, 83–9, 113–15, 125, 184
Norfolk gamekeepers, 58
Norfolk Regiment, 44
Normanton, 50
Normanby, Marquis of, 60
North, Charlie, 20
North, Commander, 70
Northampton, 117

Northamptonshire, 116–18, 150–9
North Africa, 44
North Rode, Cheshire, 114
Northumberland, 169
North Walsham, Norfolk, 113
North-West Frontier, 93
Norway, 27
Norwich, 85
Nottingham, 100
Nottinghamshire, 113, 135
Nunn, Bob, *152–3*

OCKHAM PARK, Surrey, 122–4
Oil lamps, 52
Old age, 139
Oldest keeper, 11, 27–9
Opera, 117
Orchard Portman, Somerset, 125
Orr, agent, 177
Otterden, Kent, 181
Overtoun Estate, Dumbarton, 100
Owls, 66, 92
Owlsebury, Hants, 79
Oxford, Lord, 121
Oxfordshire, 125–9

PAIN'S, JAMES, IDENTIFIERS, *168*
Palmer, John, 69
Parker, J., 48, 132
Parry-Ogden, Col, 146, 148
Partridges and partridge shooting, 16, 21, 27, 28, 29, 31, 35, 39, 44, 45, 55, *55*, 69, 70, 76, 84, 97, *102, 109*, 114, 122, 131, 148, 151, 159, 166, 167, 177
Payne-Gallwey, Sir R., *162*
Penshaw, Lambton, Durham, 66
Pensions, 132
Perks, keepers', 8, 83, 120, 121
Pesticides, 69
Petticoats, 57, 135
Pheasants and pheasant shooting, *15*, 40, 44, 55, 60, 60, 69, 76, 78, 80, 82, 97, 98, 104, *106–7*, 114, *115*, 122, 131, *134, 136, 138*, 148–9, *158*, 177
Pheasant-Tina, 33
Philip, HRH Prince, 70
Philipps, Major, 69, 70, 73
Phillips, Capt, *152–3*
Picking-up, 81
Pigeon shooting, 87, 110, 170
Pilmore, poacher, 50
Pincher, Chapman, 94
Pinkney Hall, Norfolk, 47
Pipe Line Under the Ocean (PLUTO), 80
Poachers, 11, 12, 21, 35, 45, 48–52, *49*, 56, 57, 59–60, 72, 80, 81, 85, 91, 98, 100, 104, 108, *111*, 120, 130, 132, 135–7, 140–1, 144–5, *145*, 161–2, 167–8, *169*, 175, *181–2*
Poland, 146
Pole traps, 92
Poles Walden, Herts, 143
Police, 45, 51, 52, 57, 72, 85, 98, 100, 135, 181, 182
Pollard Royal, Wilts, 166
Pollock, George, 144
Pontefract, Yorks, 48
Pool, William, 50
Portman, Lord, 125
Portsmouth, Hants, 175, 181
Postman, 164
Puckeridge Foxhounds, 17
Puddletown, Dorset, 74
Purdey guns, 110, 151
Prams, 135
Preston Candover, Hants, 83
Price, Sir Keith, 90, 92, 94
Prideaux-Brune family, 15

Pryke, George, 11, *26*, 27–9

QUEEN'S, the (Regt), 93

RABBITS, 19, 30, 31, 35, 39, 41, 50, 52, 57, *57*, 74, 82, 83, 92, 97, 110, *111*, 114, 130, 131, 144, 148, 156, 164, *164*, 180
Radziwill, Prince, 25
Railways, 66, 100, 117, 167, 172
Rationing, 129, 180
Rats, 124, 131, *131*, 156
Rearing and release, 10, 19, 27, 29, 31–4, 41–2, 44, 66, 69, 74–6, 83–4, 90, 92, 121, 122, 126, 148, 178–9, 180, 181
Rede, River, 169
References, 77
Renardine, 35
Revolvers, 72, 161–2, 165
Rheumatism, 50, 139
Rhodes, Cecil, 69
Rifles, 181
Ripley, Surrey, 122–4
Roads, 90
Roberts, poacher, 50
Robertson, jam-makers, 118
Rodd, Capt, 148, 150
Rolls Royce, 117
Romsey, Hants, 71
Romsey, Lord, 71, 138
Rooks and rook shooting, 65–6, *67*, 74, 131
Ross, John, 55
Rossyth, 179
Rowntrees, York, 37
Royal Air Force, 76, 156
Royal Artillery, 35
Royal Society for the Prevention of Cruelty to Animals, 39
Royd Moor, 48
Royal Victorian Medal, 47
Rushton, Herts, 17
Russians, 78, 109, 179
Roxburghe, Duke of, 39

SAFETY, 102
Sahara, 87
Salcey Forest, 116–18
Sales, headkeeper, 118
Salmon, 169
Sandpit Gate, 19
Sandringham, 41–7, 71, 138
Sauber, Madame, 116–18
Sawmill, 150
School, 47, 74, 113, 147, 174
Scobbie, Alexander, 144
Scotland, 70, 143, 175, 179
Scotney Castle, 122
Scott, Thomas, 66
Scythes, 62, 179
Sedgwick, Noel M., 99
Selhurst Common, Surrey, 90
Sewelling, 45, 82
Sharples, Lady, 129
Sharples, Maj Sir Richard, 129
Shaw, Walter, 148, 150
Sheikhs, 136
Sherwood Foresters, 44
Shields, keepers', 167
Shoot boundaries, 108
Shoot clothing, 38, 151
Shooting, dangerous, 70
Shooting Times, 11, 48–50, 52–3, 55, 57, 61, 71, 99, 109, *134*, 168
Shrewsbury, Shropshire, 27
Shropshire, 27–9
Shropshire Light Infantry, 44
Shropshire Yeomanry, 28
Sidebotham's traps, *173*
Signs, 56, *56*

Six Mile Bottom, 17–25, 65, 69
Skelton, headkeeper, 65
Skinning, 125, 175, 179
Sleaford, Lincs, 114
Slough of the Birnie, 143
Smithers, Harry and Herbert, 90, 91, 94
Snares, 35, 76, 141, 148
Snipe and snipe shooting, 78–80
Snow, 78, 84–5, 93, 95, 104, 131, 148
Somerset, 118–22, 125
Somme, the, 27
Sopwith, Tommy, 87, 177
South, Charles, 17–25, 18, 21, 22, 24
South, Dorcas, 25
Southampton, 72
Southwick Hall, Northants, 151, 156
Spaniels, 38–9, 53
Sparrows, 113
Sparrowhawks, 31
Special Operations Executives, 43
Spratts, 114, 115, 147, 149, 150, 162, 166, 178, 186
Sproxton, Notts, 135
Stanford, Norfolk, 12
Stand markers, 136
Stansted Park, Sussex, 181–4
Staves, 167
Stetchworth, Cambs, 25
Stoats, 27, 92, 130, 131, 175, 179
Stops, 30, 45, 90, 120, 146
Stoughton Barracks, Guildford, 93
Studley Royal, 65
Suffolk, 66–9
Survival TV films, 38
Surrey, 20–1, 90–5, 122–4
Sussex, 172–84
Sway, New Forest, 172
Swifts, 45
Swingles, 85
Swinton and Knottingley Railway, 48

TAYLOR, keeper, 169
Teal, 78, 81
Techniques, keepering, 9–10, 11
Television, 38, 146, 156
Templeton, John, 143
Terriers, 116
Territorial Army, 35, 76
Thatcher, Margaret, 122
Theory of Evolution, 94
Thetford, Suffolk, 73
Thirkill, keeper, 50
Thornham Hall, Suffolk, 66
Thrashing corn, 74, 114

Three Horseshoes pub, 54
Thunderstorms, 72, 76
Tips, keepers', 12, 21, 29, 34, 37, 39, 71–2, 78, 94, 129, 139, 151, 160, 175
Tollemache, Lord, 47
Torches, 52–3
Torrington, Viscount, 143
Tracking, 131
Transportation, 60
Traps and trapping, 33, 35, 52–3, 74, 85, 92, 113, 113, 162, 173
Tresco, Scilly Isles, 113
Trespass, 60
Truman-Mills, Henry, 85
Truman-Mills, Joseph, 83
Truncheons, 36, 72, 73
Tunis, 87
Tunisia, 87
Turkeys, 180
Turner, Thomas, headkeeper, 73
Turnworth, Dorset, 146–150

U-BOATS, 179
Uniform, keepers', 17, 20, 27, 44–5, 65, 83, 92, 118, 126, 176–7
Uppark, Sussex, 180
Utley, Mrs P., 95
Utley, Peter, 91, 94

VACANCIES, keepering, 134, 150
Van Cutsem, Hugh, 47
Vans, 133, 175, 181
Venison, 97
Vermin, 32, 33, 35, 42, 74, 77, 93, 99, 120, 124, 131, 156
Vernon, J. L., 50
Victorian keepers, 160–1
Voting, 138

WAGES, keepers', 9, 12, 17, 19, 20, 31, 37, 45, 65, 83, 87, 90, 114, 116, 118, 125, 175
Wales, 105, 129
Walker, Joseph, 164
Walsingham, Lord, 12, 162
Ward, Harry, 125–9, 127
Ware, Mrs Gertrude, 40
Ware, Stanley, 30–40, 31, 32, 35, 36, 39
Wasps, 55, 130
Watney, Combe & Reed, 20
Watson, Smoker, 66
Watson & Hancock guns, 187
Watts, keeper, 110, 110
Watts-Russell, Maj D., 156

Waugh, Police Sgt, 133
Weasels, 92, 130, 131, 131, 175
Weaver, Col, 81
Webb, Charles, 144
Welbeck, 65
Welburn, Yorks, 37
Well-diggers, 90
West, Charlie, 20
West, Jack, 86, 87
West Mersea, 167
West Newton, Norfolk, 41
Weston Colville, 21
Wheeler family, 181
Whippets, 57
Whisky, 114, 117
White, Joby, 80
Whitelaw, Lord W., 38
Whitley, Andrew, 166
Wigeon, 78
Wigmore, H., 65
Willenhall Police Court, 50
Williams, Joseph, 50
Wills, tobacco family, 118
Wilson, Jim, 152–3
Wiltshire, 70, 150, 166
Windsor, 17–25, 65
Wine, 116–17
Winkfield, Berks, 19
Wintershall, Surrey, 90–5, 95
Wisbech, 45
Wissey, River, 85
Witmore, Col, 27
Wives, keepers', 11, 77, 114–15
Wolferton, Norfolk, 47
Women's Institutes, 156
Women poachers, 57
Wood, Sir Arthur, 72
Woodcock and woodcock shooting, 63, 63, 156, 164
Woodland Pytchley Foxhunt, 156
World War I, 11, 27, 28, 30, 43, 66, 85, 147, 148
World War II, 37, 43, 44, 53, 72–3, 74, 76, 77, 80–1, 87, 90, 93, 99, 120, 121, 126, 156, 179
Wrestling, 72
Wright, Charles, 133
Wynne, poacher, 57

YARD BOY, 83
York Assizes, 60
Yorkshire, 30–40, 59–60
Young Farmers' Clubs, 156

ZETLAND, Earl of, 59

COUNTRY TITLES FROM DAVID & CHARLES

BIRDS OF PREY OF THE BRITISH ISLES · *Brian P. Martin*
COOKING WITH COUNTRY RANGES Including Aga & Rayburn · *Carol May*
DAYS & NIGHTS ON HUNTER'S FEN · *John Humphreys*
FALCONRY Care, Captive Breeding and Conservation · *Jemima Parry-Jones*
GAME COOKERY · *Angela Humphreys*
JENNIFER ALDRIDGE'S ARCHERS' COOKBOOK · *Jennifer Aldridge*
PURDEY'S The Guns and the Family · *Richard Beaumont*
SHOOTING PIGEONS · *John Humphreys*
SPORTING BIRDS OF BRITAIN & IRELAND · *Brian P. Martin*
THE COMPLETE CLAY SHOT · *Compiled by Mike Barnes*
THE COMPLETE GAME SHOOT · *John Humphreys*
THE COMPLETE GUNDOG · *John Humphreys*
THE COMPLETE ROUGH SHOOT · *John Humphreys*
THE FIELDS IN WINTER Sporting Memories of a Bygone Age · *Graham Downing*
TRAINING BIRDS OF PREY · *Jemima Parry-Jones*
WILDFOWL OF THE BRITISH ISLES AND NORTH-WEST EUROPE · *Brian P. Martin*

TALES FROM THE COUNTRYSIDE
from David & Charles

A fascinating collection of reminiscences and stories from a wide range of rural characters, recording a way of life that is rapidly disappearing. Beautifully illustrated in colour and black-and-white, these books will be treasured by anyone who loves our countryside, its wildlife and traditional crafts.

TALES OF THE OLD GAMEKEEPERS
Brian P. Martin

MORE TALES OF THE OLD GAMEKEEPERS
Brian P. Martin

TALES OF THE OLD COUNTRYMEN
Brian P. Martin

MORE TALES OF THE OLD COUNTRYMEN
Brian P. Martin

POACHERS' TALES
John Humphreys

MORE TALES OF THE OLD POACHERS
John Humphreys

TALES FROM THE WATER'S EDGE
Tom Quinn

TALES OF TIME & TIDE
Stories of Life on Britain's Shores and Coasts
Brian P. Martin

TALES OF THE OLD WOODLANDERS
Valerie Porter

TALES OF THE OLD GARDENERS
Jean Stone and Louise Brodie

TALES OF THE OLD COUNTRY FARMERS
Tom Quinn

TALES OF THE OLD COUNTRY VETS
Valerie Porter

TALES OF THE COUNTRY ECCENTRICS
Tom Quinn

TALES OF THE OLD VILLAGERS
Brian P. Martin